Written by
JUDITH FERGUSON

1509
Published in the USA 1995 by JG Press
Distributed by World Publications, Inc
Copyright © 1994 by Colour Library Books Ltd, Godalming, Surrey
All rights reserved
No part of this book may be reproduced or transmitted in any
form or by any means, electronic or mechanical, including
photocopying, recording, or by any information storage and
retrieval system, without permission in writing from the Publisher.
Printed and Bound in Singapore
ISBN 1–57215–015–7

The JG Press imprint is a trademark of JG Press, Inc.
455 Somerset Avenue
North Dighton, MA 02764

FISH & SEAFOOD

Contents

Introduction

Your fishmarket has news for you. Today, even the smallest stores have more variety than ever before. Familiar fish like cod and haddock are still around, but alongside are some very exotic creatures indeed. So much choice can be exciting, but it can be bewildering, too.

To simplify matters for culinary purposes, most saltwater and freshwater fish can be divided into four broad categories. First are the flatfish, like sole and flounder. Next are the roundfish, such as trout and bass. Third are the shellfish, oysters and lobsters for example, which all look quite different. Smoked fish, such as kippers and salmon, fall into the fourth group.

The categories of flatfish and roundfish are further subdivided into white fish and oily fish. White fish, like sole or cod can be either flat or round and have a delicate flavor and texture. They are perfect with interesting sauces or, served plain, are the most digestible of fish. Oily fish are almost always roundfish, like mackerel or herring, and have a much richer flavor. They are good broiled or baked, and combine wonderfully with spicy mustards and tangy citrus fruit.

Make friends with the people behind the fish counter and you can get good advice on which fish are in season, and thus at their best and cheapest. If you can, handle the fish. They should feel soft, but never limp. Naural slime on fish is a good indication that it is fresh, but beware of fish that feel sticky. Also, avoid fish that have dull, sunken eyes. If buying fillets, make sure the fish looks translucent. Fish should smell of the sea, but never strong and 'fishy'. Shellfish, when they are really fresh, have no smell at all.

Just as the fishmarket keeps its wares on ice, keep your purchases cold until ready to cook. Seafood deteriorates rapidly, so keep it loosely covered in plastic wrap in the refrigerator, but for no more than a day. Seafood will lose flavor and dry out in the freezer. Even if commercially frozen, seafood is best used within a week of purchase.

The methods of cooking and serving fish and shellfish are various. A whole baked fish is dramatic enough for a dinner party, broiled fish with a simple butter sauce makes a quick dinner, while shrimp and smoked fish can lift a fish pie out of the ordinary. But, rather than explain all these methods in detail, I will let the recipes speak for themselves.

Soups and Starters

Chilled Shrimp, Avocado and Cucumber Soup

PREPARATION TIME:	15 minutes
COOKING TIME:	15 minutes
SERVES:	4 people

8oz unpeeled shrimp
1 large ripe avocado
1 small cucumber
1 small bunch dill
Juice of half a lemon
1¼ cups chicken stock
2½ cups plain yogurt
Salt and pepper

Peel all shrimp, reserving shells. Add shells to chicken stock and bring to boil. Allow to simmer for about 15 minutes. Cool and strain. Peel avocado and cut it into pieces. Cut 8 thin slices from the cucumber and peel the rest. Remove seeds and chop the cucumber roughly. Put avocado and cucumber into a food processor or blender and process until smooth. Add a squeeze of lemon juice, and strain on the cold chicken stock. Reserve a sprig of dill for garnish, and add the rest to the mixture in the processor and blend again. Add about 2 cups of yogurt to the processor and blend until smooth. Add salt and pepper. Stir in peeled shrimp by hand, reserving a few as garnish. Chill soup well. Serve in individual bowls, garnished with a spoonful of yogurt, a sprig of dill, and thinly sliced rounds of cucumber.

Matelote

PREPARATION TIME:	20 minutes
COOKING TIME:	20 minutes
SERVES:	4 people

1lb sole
1lb monkfish
1 small wing of skate
1 quart mussels
8oz unpeeled shrimp
3 onions
6 tbsps butter
1⅔ cups dry cider or white wine
2 tbsps flour

2 tbsps chopped parsley
Salt
Freshly ground black pepper
Lemon juice

Fillet and skin sole. Cut fillets into large pieces. Cut monkfish similarly. Chop wing of skate into 4 large pieces. Peel shrimp and set aside. Scrub mussels well, discarding any with broken shells. Chop onion finely and soften in

half the butter. Add mussels and about 3-4 tbsps water. Cover the pan and shake over a high heat until all mussels have opened, discarding any that have not. Strain liquid into a bowl, allow mussels to cool, then shell them. Put cooking liquid back into pan. Add wine or cider, and the pieces of fish so that they are barely covered by the liquid. Simmer gently for about 8 minutes or until

This page: Chilled Shrimp, Avocado and Cucumber Soup (top) and Matelote (bottom).

Facing page: Devilled Stuffed Crab (top) and Soufflés St. Jacques (bottom).

fish is just cooked. Mix flour with remaining butter to a paste. Remove cooked fish from liquid and put into a serving dish to keep warm. Bring liquid back to boil.

Add flour and butter paste, a little at a time, whisking it in and allowing liquid to boil after each addition, until liquid is thickened. Add parsley, shelled prawns, shelled mussels, a little lemon juice, and seasoning. Heat for a few minutes to warm shellfish through. Pour over fish in serving dish and sprinkle with more chopped parsley if desired.

Devilled Stuffed Crab

PREPARATION TIME: 10-15 minutes

COOKING TIME: 20 minutes

OVEN TEMPERATURE: 375°F (190°C)

SERVES: 4 people

2 cooked crabs
¼ cup shelled pistachio nuts
2 hard-boiled eggs
1 tbsp flour
1 tbsp butter
1¼ cups milk
1 green pepper
1 medium onion
2 tbsps chili sauce or hamburger relish
2 tsps white wine vinegar
2 tsps chopped dill pickles
1 tsp Dijon mustard
½ tsp Worcestershire sauce
Tabasco
3 tbsps butter or margarine
4 tbsps dry breadcrumbs
Chopped parsley
Salt
Pepper

Garnish
Lemon wedges
Watercress

Buy the crabs already cleaned. If you wish to do it yourself, twist off all the legs, separate body from shell, and remove lungs and stomach. Cut body into 3 or 4 pieces with a sharp knife and pick out all the meat. Scrape brown meat from inside shell; crack large claws and remove meat, adding add all this meat to the body meat. Crab shells may be washed and used to bake in. Prepare cream sauce. Melt 1 tbsp butter in a small saucepan. When foaming, take it off the heat and stir in flour, then the milk, gradually. Mix well. Return to heat and bring to boil, allowing it to thicken. Set aside to cool slightly. Chop egg roughly, and green pepper and onion into small dice. Break up crabmeat roughly. Chop pistachio nuts, and add all other ingredients to the white sauce. Lightly butter the clean shell

or individual baking dishes. Fill with crabmeat mixture and top with dry crumbs. Melt 3 tbsps butter and sprinkle over top of crumbs. Bake for 15 minutes, and brown under broiler if necessary. Sprinkle with chopped parsley and garnish with watercress and lemon wedges.

Soufflés St. Jacques

PREPARATION TIME: 20 minutes

COOKING TIME: 20 minutes

OVEN TEMPERATURE: 450°F (225°C)

SERVES: 4 people

8 large or 16 small scallops, with roe attached (if possible)
1¼ cups milk
2½ tbsps butter
2½ tbsps flour
2½ tbsps grated Cheddar cheese
4 eggs
Salt
Pepper
¼ tsp Dijon mustard

Tomato Sauce
1¾ cups canned tomatoes
1 small onion, finely chopped
Bay leaf
Pinch of thyme
Sugar
Half a clove of garlic, crushed
1 tbsp Worcestershire sauce
Salt
Pepper

First prepare tomato sauce. Combine onion with rest of the ingredients in a small, heavy saucepan. Bring to the boil, then lower heat, leaving to simmer, half-covered, for 20 minutes. Strain the sauce and set aside. Poach scallops in milk for about 5 minutes. Remove from milk and set aside. Melt butter in a small saucepan, and when foaming remove from heat, and stir in flour. Add milk in which scallops were poached. Bring to the boil, stirring constantly until thickened. Add salt and pepper, then stir in the grated cheese. Leave to cool slightly. Separate eggs, beat the yolks and add them to cheese sauce. Butter 4 deep scallop shells or porcelain baking dishes. Slice scallops through the middle, horizontally. Reserve 1 whole roe per serving. Place scallops in bottom of the shells. Beat egg whites until stiff but not dry, and fold into cheese mixture. Divide soufflé mixture between the scallop shells, and place them on a baking tray. Bake in a hot oven for about 10 minutes or until well

risen. Meanwhile, re-heat tomato sauce and spoon some of it, when scallops are ready, into each dish. Serve remaining tomato sauce separately. Garnish each serving with the reserved whole roe.

Garlic Fried Scallops

PREPARATION TIME: 10 minutes

COOKING TIME: 6-8 minutes

SERVES: 4 people

16 scallops
1 large clove garlic, peeled and chopped finely
4 tbsps butter
3 tbsps chopped parsley
2 lemons
Seasoned flour

Rinse scallops and remove black veins. If scallops are large, cut in half horizontally. Squeeze the juice from 1 lemon. Sprinkle scallops lightly with seasoned flour. Heat butter in a frying pan and add chopped garlic and scallops. Fry until pale golden brown. Pour over lemon juice, and cook to reduce the amount of liquid. Toss in the chopped parsley. Pile scallops into individual scallop shells or porcelain baking dishes. Keep warm, and garnish with lemon wedges before serving.

Langoustine and Avocado Cocktail

PREPARATION TIME: 20 minutes

SERVES: 4 people

8oz cooked langoustines or large shrimp
2 oranges
2 large, ripe avocados
1 small red onion or 2 green onions
¼ cup whipping cream
2 tbsps ketchup
2 tbsps mayonnaise
2 tsps lemon juice
12 (approx) black olives, stoned and sliced
2 tsps brandy
Pinch of Cayenne pepper
Pinch sugar
Salt
Freshly ground pepper
Lettuce

Peel oranges over a bowl to reserve juice. Peel cooked langoustines and set aside. To prepare dressing, whip cream until thick, and mix with ketchup, mayonnaise, lemon juice, Cayenne, sugar, salt and pepper,

brandy and some of the reserved orange juice to let down to the proper consistency – the dressing should be slightly thick. Chop onion finely. Cut avocados in half lengthwise and take out stones. Peel them carefully and cut each half into 4-6 long slices. Shred lettuce and put onto serving dishes. Arrange avocado slices in a fan shape on top of the lettuce. Brush each slice lightly with orange juice to keep green. Arrange an orange segment in between each slice. Pile langoustines up at the top of the avocado fan and coat with some of the dressing. Garnish with olives and sprinkle over chopped onion.

Quenelles au Beurre Blanc

PREPARATION TIME: 25 minutes

COOKING TIME: 20 minutes

SERVES: 4 people

1lb pike or other white fish
2 cups white breadcrumbs
4 tbsps milk
6 tbsps butter
2 eggs
Salt
Pepper
Nutmeg
Cayenne pepper

Beurre Blanc Sauce
½ cup unsalted butter
1 small onion, peeled and chopped finely
1 tbsp white wine vinegar
2 tbsps lemon juice
3 tbsps dry white wine
1 tsp snipped chives
Salt

Vegetable Garnish
1 medium zucchini, topped and tailed
1 leek, trimmed, with some green attached
1 carrot, peeled
1 stick celery, washed and trimmed

First prepare quenelle mixture. Skin and bone fish and cut into small pieces. Place in a food processor bowl. Soak the breadcrumbs in milk; drain away most of the liquid, and put into the food processor with the fish. Melt butter and pour into the fish mixture with the machine running. Work mixture to a smooth purée. Add eggs, continuing to mix until smooth. Add salt and pepper, cayenne pepper and nutmeg. Chill mixture in refrigerator for at least 1 hour, or overnight.

Garlic Fried Scallops (right) and Langoustine and Avocado Cocktail (below).

To cook quenelles, fill a sauté pan with salted water. Bring to the boil. Reduce heat until water is just simmering. With two spoons, shape quenelles into little ovals. Poach them in water for about 6 minutes, turning them over about half way through. Remove them with a slotted spoon. Drain and put them in a dish to keep warm in the oven, covered. To prepare beurre blanc sauce, put chopped onion into a small saucepan with the vinegar and wine. Bring to boil and allow to reduce by half. Remove pan from heat, and allow to cool a little. Cut butter into small pieces and add to onion mixture, a little at a time, whisking well to a creamy sauce. After 2-3 pieces have been added, place pan back over low heat and continue whisking until all butter has been added. Season the sauce, add lemon juice, strain, add the snipped chives and serve hot over quenelles.

To prepare garnish, cut all vegetables into 2″ lengths, then cut those into thin strips. Bring water in a large saucepan to the boil, with a pinch of salt. Cook carrots for about 5 minutes. Then add celery strips and cook for another 5 minutes. Add zucchini and leek, and cook for 3 minutes more. Drain vegetables well, add them to the sauce and pour over the quenelles to serve.

Cucumbers and Shrimp

PREPARATION TIME: 20 minutes

SERVES: 4 people

1 large or 2 small cucumbers
8oz unpeeled shrimp
¼ cup heavy cream
¼ cup plain yogurt
½ tsp Dijon mustard
Juice of 1 lemon
1 tbsp chopped parsley
Pinch sugar
Large bunch of chervil, chopped, but reserving some whole for garnish
1 head of red chicory
1 head of Romaine lettuce
Salt and pepper

Peel cucumber and slice in half lengthwise. Scoop out seeds and cut each half into thin slices. Sprinkle slices with salt and leave to drain for about 1 hour. Peel shrimp, reserving 4 unpeeled for garnish. Whip cream lightly and fold together with yogurt, mustard, 1 tsp of the lemon juice, parsley and chervil. Add seasoning and sugar, and mix the dressing together with the shrimp. Wash salt from cucumber, and dry slices well. Divide lettuce and chicory between 4 serving plates and toss cucumber together with the shrimp. Peel shells from the tails of the reserved shrimp, and set aside. Pile cucumber and shrimp mixture onto lettuce leaves and garnish with reserved shrimp and whole sprigs of chervil.

Mussels in Lemon Cream

PREPARATION TIME: 10 minutes

COOKING TIME: 10 minutes

SERVES: 4 people

1 quart mussels
Grated rind and juice of 2 lemons
1 shallot, finely chopped
1¼ cups heavy cream
2 tbsps chopped parsley
Flour or oatmeal
2 tbsps butter

Scrub mussels well, discarding any with broken shells. Put into a bowl with clean, cold water, and add a handful of flour or oatmeal. Leave for ½ hour, then drain mussels under clean water. Put the butter and finely chopped shallot into a large pan and cook until shallot is soft, but not colored. Add lemon juice, then mussels. Cover and cook quickly, shaking the pan until mussel shells open. Discard any that do not open. Remove mussels and keep them warm. Strain the liquid and return it to the rinsed-out pan. Add the cream and bring to the boil. Allow to boil for 5 minutes to thicken slightly. Pour over the mussels, and sprinkle grated lemon rind and chopped parsley over.

This page: Cucumbers and Shrimp (top) and Quenelles au Beurre Blanc (bottom).
Facing page: Marinated Smoked Fish (top) and Mussels in Lemon Cream (bottom).

Marinated Smoked Fish

PREPARATION TIME: 10 minutes, plus 1 hour to marinate

SERVES: 4 people

1 kippered herring
4oz smoked salmon
1 large fillet of smoked sable
1 large whole smoked trout
¼ cup vegetable oil
Juice of 1 large lemon

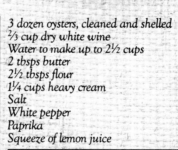

Cook fishbones in water with the carrot, celery and onion. Add bay leaf, and simmer for about 1 hour. Drain off stock and reserve. Add tomatoes to stock. Chop spring onions, pickles, olives and capers. Cut salmon into 1" cubes, add to stock, season and cover. Simmer for 10-12 minutes or until salmon is cooked. Put soup into warm serving dishes and top with sour cream and black caviar.

Oyster Bisque

PREPARATION TIME: 10 minutes
COOKING TIME: 27 minutes
SERVES: 4 people

3 dozen oysters, cleaned and shelled
⅔ cup dry white wine
Water to make up to 2½ cups
2 tbsps butter
2½ tbsps flour
1¼ cups heavy cream
Salt
White pepper
Paprika
Squeeze of lemon juice

Chop oysters roughly, reserving 4 for garnish. Put chopped oysters and their liquid into a medium saucepan with the water and wine. Bring to boil and allow to simmer for 15 minutes. Blend, and measure the amount of liquid. Reduce, or add water, to make 1 pint. Melt 1½ tbsps butter in a saucepan and when foaming, remove from heat and add flour. Cook flour and butter together for about 1 minute until very pale brown. Add oyster liquid gradually.
Stir well, bring back to boil and simmer gently for about 10 minutes. Season with salt, a pinch of paprika and a good pinch of white pepper. Add heavy cream, return to heat and allow to boil for 1-2 minutes. Add lemon juice, if desired. Cook reserved oysters

1 tbsp white wine vinegar
1 red onion, sliced
Lettuce
Parsley
Salt and pepper

Remove skin from kipper and sable, and cut each into 8 pieces. Fillet and skin the trout, and cut each fillet into 4 pieces. Shred the smoked salmon. Put fish into a large, shallow dish. Scatter onion slices on top of the fish. Mix oil, lemon juice and vinegar together. Add salt and pepper, and pour over fish. Leave to marinate for at least 1

hour. Serve on a bed of lettuce with some of the onions from the marinade, and chopped parsley. Other varieties of smoked fish may be substituted.

Solianka

PREPARATION TIME: 10 minutes
COOKING TIME: 1 hour
10 minutes
SERVES: 4 people

2lbs fish bones

1½lbs salmon or salmon trout
1¼ cups canned tomatoes
5 cups water
1 onion, roughly chopped
1 stick celery, roughly chopped
1 carrot, roughly chopped
1 small bunch green onions
4 small dill pickles
2 tbsps capers
1 tbsp chopped black olives
1 bay leaf
Salt and pepper
⅔ cup sour cream

Garnish
1 small jar black caviar

quickly in remaining butter. Put soup into warm serving dishes. Top each with 1 oyster and a sprinkling of paprika.

Mussels alla Genovese

PREPARATION TIME: 15 minutes
COOKING TIME: 5-8 minutes
SERVES: 4 people

1 quart mussels
Lemon juice
1 shallot, finely chopped
1 handful fresh basil leaves
1 small bunch parsley
4-5 walnut halves
1 clove garlic
2 tbsps freshly grated Parmesan cheese
3-6 tbsps olive oil
2 tbsps butter

Solianka (above), Oyster Bisque (right) and Mussels alla Genovese.

1 small jar red caviar
Salt
Pepper
Tabasco

Garnish
Watercress

Open oysters and leave them in their half-shells. Put a drop of Tabasco on each oyster, season, then 2 tsps of heavy cream. Melt butter and sprinkle it over oysters. Put them under a hot broiler for 2-3 minutes. When cooked, top each one with 1 tsp red caviar, and serve hot with bouquets of watercress as garnish.

Green Beans, Hazelnuts and Langoustines

PREPARATION TIME:	15 minutes
COOKING TIME:	19-21 minutes
OVEN TEMPERATURE:	350°F (180°C)
SERVES:	4 people

1lb green beans, trimmed
¾lb cooked langoustines or large shrimp
¼ cup whole hazelnuts, skinned
1 red pepper, stem and seeds removed, and sliced thinly
⅓ cup olive oil
3 tbsps white wine vinegar
1 tsp Dijon mustard
1 tbsp chopped parsley
1 small head iceberg lettuce, shredded
Salt
Pepper

Toast hazelnuts in moderate oven for about 15 minutes or until golden brown. Allow to cool. Chop roughly. Bring salted water to the boil in a saucepan, and cook beans in it for about 4-6 minutes – they should remain crisp. Drain, refresh under cold water, drain again and dry. Cook pepper slices in boiling water for about 1 minute. Drain and refresh under cold water, and allow to dry. Whisk oil, vinegar, Dijon mustard and seasonings together. Peel

Salt and pepper
Flour or oatmeal

Garnish
Fresh bay leaves or basil leaves

Scrub the mussels well and discard any with broken shells. Put mussels into a bowl of clean water with a handful of flour or oatmeal. Leave for ½ hour, then rinse under clear water. Chop shallot finely and put into a large saucepan with lemon juice. Cook until shallot softens. Add mussels and a pinch of salt and pepper. Cover the pan and cook the mussels quickly, shaking the pan. When mussel shells have

opened, take mussels out of the pan, set aside and keep warm. Strain the cooking liquid for possible use later. To prepare Genovese sauce, wash the basil leaves and parsley, peel the garlic clove and chop roughly, and chop the walnuts roughly. Put the herbs, garlic, nuts, 1 tbsp grated cheese and salt and pepper into a food processor and work to chop roughly. Add butter and work again. Turn machine on and add oil gradually through the feed tube. If the sauce is still too thick, add the reserved liquid from cooking the mussels. Remove top shells from mussels and discard. Arrange

mussels evenly in 4 shallow dishes, spoon some of the sauce into each, and sprinkle the top lightly with remaining Parmesan cheese. Garnish with bay or basil leaves and serve.

Broiled Oysters

PREPARATION TIME:	10 minutes
COOKING TIME:	2-3 minutes
SERVES:	4 people

2 doz oysters
4 tbsps butter
1¼ cups heavy cream

**This page: Devilled Whitebait (Smelts) (top) and Green Beans, Hazelnuts and Langoustines (bottom).
Facing page: Broiled Oysters (top) and Crab and Citrus (bottom).**

langoustines, and mix together with beans, pepper, hazelnuts and dressing. Arrange lettuce on individual serving dishes, and pile remaining ingredients on top. Sprinkle parsley over the top to serve.

Smoked Salmon Stuffed Cucumbers

PREPARATION TIME: 15 minutes

SERVES: 4 people

4oz smoked salmon
1 8oz package cream cheese
1 large cucumber
1 head iceberg lettuce
1 bunch chives
1 bunch dill
⅔ cup plain yogurt
2 tbsps whipping cream
Squeeze of lemon juice
Salt
Pepper

Garnish
1 tsp red salmon caviar

Peel cucumber and trim off the ends. Cut in half lengthwise and scoop out the seeds. Sprinkle the surface with salt and leave on paper towels for 1 hour. Meanwhile, prepare the filling. Work the smoked salmon and the cream cheese in a food processor until smooth. Snip the chives and stir in by hand. Prepare the dressing by mixing the yogurt, whipping cream and finely chopped dill together with salt, pepper and lemon juice to taste. Rinse and dry the cucumber very well. Using a pastry bag fitted with a ½″ plain tube, fill the bag with the smoked salmon mixture and pipe the filling into the hollow left in the cucumber. Put the other half on top, press together firmly, and wrap tightly in plastic wrap. Chill in the refrigerator for 1 hour. Separate the lettuce leaves, wash and dry well, and place on individual serving dishes. Unwrap the cucumber and slice into ½″ slices. Place on top of lettuce. Spoon over some of the dressing and top with caviar. Serve the rest of the dressing separately.

Devilled Whitebait (Smelt)

PREPARATION TIME: 10 minutes

COOKING TIME: 5-6 minutes

SERVES: 4 people

1lb whitebait (smelt)
Flour
Salt
Pepper
¼ tsp Cayenne pepper
¼ tsp dry mustard
1 large pinch ground ginger
Paprika
Oil for deep frying

Garnish
Lemon wedges
Parsley

Pick over, but do not wash, fish. Mix flour with salt, pepper, Cayenne, ginger and mustard, and roll whitebait in mixture until lightly coated. Heat oil in deep-fat fryer to 350°F (180°C). Put small amount of floured fish into frying basket, lower into the fat, and fry for 2-3 minutes. Drain on crumpled paper towels. Sprinkle lightly with salt, and continue until all fish are fried. Re-heat fat, and add all fish. Fry for 1-2 minutes until crisp. Turn out onto hot serving dish. Sprinkle with salt and paprika. Serve at once with lemon wedges and bouquets of parsley.

Crab and Citrus

PREPARATION TIME: 20 minutes

SERVES: 4 people

8oz crabmeat, or 1 large crab
2 oranges
2 lemons
2 limes
1 pink grapefruit
1 small iceberg lettuce
⅔ cup plain yogurt
⅓ cup heavy cream
1 tbsp chili sauce
½ tbsp brandy
Pinch of Cayenne pepper
Salt
2 tbsps salad oil

Separate body from shell of whole crab, and remove and discard lungs and stomach sac. Chop body into 3 or 4 pieces with a very sharp knife and pick out the meat. Scrape brown meat from inside shell and add to body meat. Break off large claws and remove meat from legs; then crack the claws and remove claw meat. Mix all meat together and reserve legs for garnish. (If using canned or frozen crabmeat, pick over the meat to remove any bits of shell or cartilage.) Mix together yogurt, chili sauce, cream, brandy, Cayenne pepper and a pinch of salt, and toss with the crabmeat. Take a thin strip of peel from each of the citrus fruits, scraping off the bitter white pith.

Cut each strip of peel into thin slivers. Put into boiling water and allow to boil for about 1 minute. Drain, refresh under cold water, and set aside. Peel each of the citrus fruits and cut into segments; do all this over a bowl to reserve juices. Add 2 tbsps salad oil to the juice in the bowl, and toss with citrus segments. Shred iceberg lettuce and arrange on plates. Put the crabmeat in its dressing on top of lettuce. Arrange citrus segments over and around crabmeat and sprinkle citrus peel over the top.

Lobster à la Creme

PREPARATION TIME: 10 minutes

COOKING TIME: 5 minutes

SERVES: 4 people

1 cold, boiled lobster
1¼ cups heavy cream
4 tbsps butter
¼ cup dry sherry or Madeira
Squeeze of lemon juice
Ground nutmeg
3 tbsps dry breadcrumbs
1 small bunch of tarragon, chopped
Salt and pepper

Cut lobster in half lengthwise with a sharp knife. Remove meat from tail. Crack claws and remove meat. Remove as much meat as possible from all the legs. Chop all meat roughly. Melt 3 tbsps of the butter in a sauté pan and sauté the lobster with the seasonings, lemon juice, nutmeg and tarragon. Flame the sherry or Madeira and pour over the lobster in the sauté pan. Shake the pan until flames die out. Pour over heavy cream and bring to the boil. Allow to boil for 5 minutes until cream begins to thicken. Spoon into individual serving dishes. Melt remaining butter in a small frying pan and brown the dry breadcrumbs. When golden brown and crisp, sprinkle over the top of lobster.

Shrimp and Watercress Bisque

PREPARATION TIME: 20 minutes

COOKING TIME: 25 minutes

SERVES: 4 people

2½ cups plain yogurt
2 medium potatoes
½ clove garlic
2 bunches watercress
butter
8oz cod or other white fish
16 (approx) unpeeled shrimp

Milk
Salt
White pepper

Shell all the shrimp, and reserve shells. Place cod in a pan with enough water to cover. Bring to boil, reduce heat and allow to simmer for about 5 minutes. Remove fish from pan and peel the skin away. Reserve the liquid. Return cod skin to pan with the shells from the shrimp. Cook for a few minutes and leave to cool. Meanwhile, peel and cook potatoes until tender, and mash with a little milk and the butter. Pick over watercress, discarding any yellow leaves and root ends. Reserve small sprigs of leaves for garnish and chop the rest roughly. Reserve 4 tbsps yogurt per serving for garnish. Put remaining yogurt, potatoes, salt, pepper, garlic and watercress into the bowl of a food processor. Add skinned cod and strain in fish liquid, discarding skin and shrimp shells. Work until to the consistency of thick cream, using as much milk as necessary. When soup is smooth and desired consistency is reached, put into a clean saucepan and warm gently – do not allow to boil. Put into warm soup bowls or tureen to serve. Garnish with a spoonful of yogurt, peeled shrimp and watercress leaves.

Chinese Crabmeat Soup

PREPARATION TIME: 10 minutes

COOKING TIME: 10 minutes

SERVES: 4 people

4oz crabmeat
Small piece fresh ginger
2 tbsps light soy sauce
2¾ cups light chicken stock
4 green onions
1 piece of to-fu or soy bean curd, well drained
2 tsps cornstarch
1 tsp sesame seed oil
1 tbsp dry sherry
Salt
Pepper

Smoked Salmon Stuffed
Cucumbers (below) and
Lobster á la Creme (bottom).

Heat oil in medium-sized saucepan, and fry crabmeat for about a minute. Peel and grate ginger, and add it to pan with sherry, salt and pepper and soy sauce. Stir together and add stock, reserving about 2 tbsps to mix with the cornstarch. Bring soup to boil. Add a little of the boiling liquid to the cornstarch mixture, then add to the soup. Stir until slightly thickened. Slice green onions on a slant and add to soup. Slice bean curd into ½″ cubes, add to the soup, and heat through with the sesame seed oil. Serve.

Soupe de Poisson Provençal

PREPARATION TIME:	20 minutes
COOKING TIME:	30-40 minutes
SERVES:	4 people

Soup
3lbs white fish
8oz shrimp
1 large onion
2 leeks
5 cups canned tomatoes
2 cloves garlic
1 bay leaf
1 sprig thyme
1 small piece fennel or 2 parsley stalks
2 pinches saffron
Strip of orange rind
⅔ cup white wine
2 tbsps butter
2 tbsps flour
⅔ cup olive oil
5 cups water
Salt
Pepper
Tomato paste
Cream

Sauce Rouille
½ cup chopped red pepper or canned pimento
1 small chili pepper
3-4 tbsps fresh breadcrumbs
3 cloves garlic
1 egg yolk
⅔ cup olive oil
Salt
Pepper

Accompaniment
Grated Parmesan cheese
Croûtons

First prepare soup. Chop onion. Clean and chop leeks, and cook them slowly, with the onion, in the olive oil until tender, but not browned. Mash garlic cloves and add to leeks and onion, along with the canned tomatoes. Bring to the boil and cook for 5 minutes. Meanwhile, skin and bone fish, shell shrimp , and tie the bay leaf, thyme, fennel and orange peel together with a small piece of string. Put the water, wine, the bundle of herbs, the saffron, salt and pepper, fish and shellfish into the pan and cook, uncovered, on a moderate heat for 30-40 minutes. Meanwhile, prepare Sauce Rouille. Cut chili pepper in half and rinse out seeds. Use half or all, depending on desired hotness. Chop chili pepper together with sweet red pepper. Peel and chop garlic. Soak breadcrumbs in water and press them dry. Put peppers, breadcrumbs, garlic and egg yolk into a blender with a pinch of salt and pepper and blend to a smooth paste, or work together with mortar and pestle. Gradually add oil in a thin, steady stream. The consistency should be that of mayonnaise. Set aside. When soup is cooked, remove the bundle of herbs. Put contents of soup pan into the food processor and work to a smooth purée. Strain if necessary, correct seasoning, and add some tomato paste for color, if necessary. Return to saucepan. Mix butter and flour into a paste. Add about 1 tsp of the paste to the soup, whisking it in well, and bring the soup up to the boil. Add more paste as necessary to bring the soup to the consistency of thick cream. Stir in the cream. Serve soup with the rouille, cheese and croûtons.

This page: Soupe de Poisson Provençal.
Facing page: Chinese Crabmeat Soup (top) and Shrimp and Watercress Bisque (bottom).

Pâtés, Terrines and Mousses

Smoked Trout Pâté

PREPARATION TIME: 20 minutes

SERVES: 4 people

4 lemons
2 fillets or 1 whole smoked trout
6 tbsps butter
8oz package cream cheese
Lemon juice
Tabasco
Ground nutmeg
Salt
Pepper

Garnish
Fresh bay leaves

Cut lemons in half and trim the ends so the shells sit upright. Scoop out the lemon flesh completely. Remove skin and bones from trout. Put fish into a food processor with the butter, cream cheese, seasoning, lemon juice, nutmeg and Tabasco. Work until smooth. Put the pâté into a pastry bag fitted with a rose tube and pipe into the lemon shells. Garnish each with a bay leaf. Serve with hot toast.

Pâté of Salmon and Scallops

PREPARATION TIME: 30 minutes

COOKING TIME: 1 hour

OVEN TEMPERATURE: 350°F (180°C)

SERVES: 4 people

¾lb salmon
1lb haddock or other white fish
5 scallops with roe attached
1¼ cups heavy cream
3 eggs
1 tbsp chopped parsley
1 tbsp chopped fresh tarragon
1 tbsp lemon juice
1 tbsp dry white wine
½ cup unsalted butter
Salt
Pepper
Pinch Cayenne pepper

Separate eggs and set aside yolks. Remove skin and bone from haddock and salmon. Put salmon

into a food processor bowl with half the egg whites and half the cream. Season and process until smooth. Put into separate bowl, and repeat the process with the haddock. Lightly butter a 2lb loaf pan. Put half of haddock mixture into the bottom of the pan and smooth out. Cover with half of the

salmon mixture. Clean scallops and separate roe from white part. Cut white part in half through the middle. Chop roe roughly and put it down the center of the salmon mixture. Place the rounds of white scallops on either side of the roe. Put another layer of salmon mixture over, and then the

**This page: Pâté of Salmon and Scallops (top) and Kippered Fish Mousse (bottom).
Facing page: Smoked Trout Pâté (top) and Crabmeat Mousse (bottom).**

remaining haddock mixture on top and smooth out. Cover well with double thickness of buttered foil. Put into a roasting pan and fill it halfway up with hand-hot water. Bake pâté in oven for about 1 hour. Meanwhile, prepare a quick Bernaise sauce. Put reserved egg yolks into a food processor bowl or blender. Chop herbs roughly and add to egg yolks along with Cayenne pepper, pinch of salt, lemon juice and white wine. Process until mixed thoroughly and the herbs are chopped. Melt butter and, when foaming, turn on machine and pour the melted butter through feed tube very gradually. This will cook the egg yolks and the sauce will thicken. Keep warm in a double boiler. When pâté has finished cooking, allow to cool slightly in the pan. Gently turn fish pâté out and cut into 1″ thick slices. Arrange on serving plates and pour over some of the Bernaise sauce. Serve the rest of the sauce separately.

Smoked Salmon Mousse

PREPARATION TIME: 20 minutes

COOKING TIME: 5 minutes

SERVES: 4 people

¾lb smoked salmon
2½ cups prepared mayonnaise
1 tbsp powdered gelatine
Lemon juice
¼ cup heavy cream
1 tbsp flour
1 tbsp butter
¾ cup milk
1 egg white
1 small cucumber
1 jar red caviar
1 bunch watercress
1 small head iceberg lettuce
Salt and pepper

Lightly oil ramekin dishes or small individual molds. Mix lemon juice with enough water to make 3 tbsps, and dissolve gelatine in the liquid. Warm gelatine through gently to melt. Prepare sauce by melting butter and, when foaming, adding flour. Stir together well and blend in the milk gradually. Put back on the heat and bring to the boil to thicken. Allow to cool slightly. Chop the smoked salmon roughly and put into a food processor bowl with half the prepared mayonnaise. Add seasonings and prepared sauce. Process until smooth and, with machine still running, pour in the melted gelatine. Pour in cream and process briefly. Set mixture over ice

or in a cool place until thickening. When thickened, whisk egg white until stiff but not dry, and fold into salmon mousse mixture. Put mixture into individual molds and chill until firm. Meanwhile, prepare green mayonnaise. Pick over the watercress leaves, wash them well, remove thick stalks and the root ends. Chop roughly and put into food processor bowl. Add remaining prepared mayonnaise, seasonings and lemon juice to taste, and process until well blended and a good green color. Spread mayonnaise onto individual serving plates. When mousse is chilled and set, turn out on top of green mayonnaise. Garnish the plate with shredded lettuce. Garnish the top of each mousse with a thin slice of cucumber and a little red caviar.

Crabmeat Mousse

PREPARATION TIME: 30 minutes

SERVES: 4 people

1lb crabmeat, cooked and flaked
⅓ cup prepared mayonnaise
⅔ cup whipping cream
2 tbsps sherry
2 egg whites
2 tsps Dijon mustard
1 small bunch chives
1 tbsp commercial aspic powder
Juice of 1 lime or lemon
1 ripe avocado
1 tbsp gelatine
Salt and pepper

Dissolve gelatine in some of the lemon or lime juice. Warm gently to dissolve, and mix with mayonnaise, mustard, and salt and pepper to taste. Lightly whip the cream and fold into mayonnaise mixture along with crabmeat. Put over ice or in a cool place until thickened, then whisk the egg whites until stiff but not dry, and fold into mixture. Quickly pour into a bowl or soufflé dish, smooth the top and chill until set. Meanwhile, bring 1 cup water to boil. Stir in sherry, add 1 tbsp commercial aspic powder and stir until dissolved. Allow to cool slightly. Chop chives and add to aspic. When mousse mixture is set, chill aspic until it begins to thicken slightly. Pour about ¼″ of the aspic over the top of the set mousse, and return to refrigerator to set the aspic. Cut avocado in half lengthwise and remove stone. Peel carefully and cut each half into thin slices. Brush with lemon juice and arrange slices on top of set aspic.

Spoon over some of the aspic to set the avocado slices, and chill. When avocado is set, pour remaining aspic over to fill to the top of dish, and chill until set.

Kippered Fish Mousse

PREPARATION TIME: 20 minutes

SERVES: 4 people

6 small or 3 large kippered herrings
¾ cup heavy cream
⅔ cup prepared mayonnaise
1 tbsp brandy
1 tbsp grated horseradish
½ clove garlic
1 shallot, finely chopped
1 tbsp powdered gelatine
Salt
Pepper
Lemon juice
Vegetable oil

Garnish
Sliced cucumbers
Sliced lemon
Chives

Skin kippers and remove any bones. Mix lemon juice with water to make 3 tbsps. Dissolve gelatine in this liquid, and heat gently to melt gelatine. Put fillets into food processor with brandy, mayonnaise, salt, pepper, garlic, and finely chopped shallot. Work until smooth, then, with the machine running, pour the liquid gelatine through feed tube to blend. Put mixture over ice or in a cool place until it begins to thicken. Lightly whip cream and fold into thickened mousse mixture. Lightly oil a mold with vegetable oil. Pour in the mousse mixture. Smooth down and tap to remove any air bubbles. Chill overnight, or until set. Turn out onto a serving plate and surround with a garnish of thinly sliced cucumbers, and thinly sliced lemons. Chives may be used to decorate the mold if desired.

Tricolor Terrine

PREPARATION TIME: 25 minutes

COOKING TIME: 15 minutes

SERVES: 4 people

4oz smoked haddock (finnan haddie)
4oz fresh haddock or other white fish
1 large kippered herring
⅔ cup prepared mayonnaise
2 tbsps flour
2 tbsps butter

1¼ cups milk
1 tbsp chopped parsley
3 tbsps heavy cream
1 tbsp gelatine
1 egg white
Juice of 1 lemon
⅔ cup sour cream
1 tbsp grated horseradish
1 bunch dill, reserving 4 small sprigs
Iceberg lettuce
Watercress

Poach smoked haddock in water and half the milk to cover for 10 minutes. Skin and remove any bones. Cook fresh haddock separately, using fresh water and the remaining milk. Skin kippered herring. Mash the fish well, or work in a food processor, keeping each fish separate. Prepare the sauce by melting the butter, adding flour off the heat. Stir in the cooking liquid from the fish and put the sauce back onto the heat. Stir until boiling, then season well. Soak gelatine in 1 tbsp lemon juice plus enough water to make 3 tbsps. Melt over gentle heat until dissolved. Whip cream lightly until it just holds its shape. Put haddock, smoked haddock and kipper in separate bowls. Divide sauce, gelatine and mayonnaise equally between each bowl. Mix together

together for the sauce, and season well. When the tureen is set, turn out of the pan and slice into ¾" thick slices. Place on a serving plate with a garnish of lettuce, watercress and reserved dill, and a spoonful of the horseradish sauce. Serve the rest of the horseradish sauce separately.

well and fold in the heavy cream, similarly divided. Lightly oil a 1lb loaf pan. Set the mixtures in a cool place until thickening and, when starting to thicken, whip the egg white. Divide that equally into the fish mixtures. Put smoked haddock mixture into the bottom of the loaf pan and smooth out. Spoon the fresh haddock over the smoked haddock mixture and spread out on top. Spoon kipper mixture on top of that, and level out. Chill in the refrigerator until well set. Mix sour cream, horseradish, chopped dill, chopped parsley, and lemon

Cold Dishes and Salads

Salad Niçoise

PREPARATION TIME: 20 minutes

COOKING TIME: 15-20 minutes

SERVES: 4 people

1 can tuna
4oz shrimp
6-8 anchovies
4 ripe tomatoes
4 hard-boiled eggs
1 red pepper
½ cup black olives, stoned
1 cup green beans
2 large potatoes, or 6 small new
    potatoes
2 tbsps white wine vinegar
6 tbsps olive oil
3 tbsps chopped mixed herbs
1 tbsp Dijon mustard
Salt and pepper

Peel and cook potatoes (skins may be left on new potatoes if desired) until tender. If using large potatoes, cut into ½" dice (new potatoes may be sliced into ¼" rounds). Trim beans, put into boiling salted water for about 3-4 minutes or until just barely cooked. Drain and rinse under cold water, then leave to drain dry. Cut the olives in half, lengthwise. Cut anchovies in half, lengthwise, then through the middle. Cut tomatoes into quarters (or eighths, if large) and remove the cores. Mix the vinegar and oil together for the vinaigrette dressing, and add seasoning, chopped herbs, and a little French mustard if desired. Drain oil from tuna fish. Cut red pepper into thin shreds. Mix together all the ingredients, including the shrimp, and toss in the dressing. Quarter the eggs and toss into the other ingredients very carefully – do not break up the eggs. Pile onto dishes and serve.

Spanish Rice and Sole Salad

PREPARATION TIME: 20 minutes

COOKING TIME: 8-10 minutes

OVEN TEMPERATURE:
350°F (180°C)

SERVES: 4 people

2 sole filleted and skinned
4-6 peppercorns
Slice of onion
Lemon juice
5 tbsps olive oil
1 cup long-grain rice
1 red pepper
1 shallot, finely chopped
1 small eggplant
1 green pepper

2 bunches watercress
1¼ cups prepared mayonnaise
1 clove garlic
1 level tsp tomato paste
1 level tsp paprika
1 tbsp chopped mixed herbs
Salt and pepper

Put sole fillets into a baking dish. Add onion, a squeeze of lemon

This page: Marinated Herring in Sour Cream with Beet Salad. Facing page: Salad Niçoise (top) and Spanish Rice and Sole Salad (bottom).

juice, peppercorns and enough
water to cover. Sprinkle with salt,
cover with buttered foil, and bake
in a moderate oven for about 8-10
minutes. Allow fish to cool in the
liquid, then cut into 1" pieces.
Cook rice for about 12 minutes.
Drain under hot water, then cold,
and leave to drain completely dry.
Chop green and red peppers into
¼" dice. Cut eggplant in half
lengthwise, score each half, sprinkle
with salt, and leave to sit for about
½ hour. Wash eggplant well, then
dry it. Cut it into ½" cubes and fry
very quickly in 2 tbsps olive oil.

Add salt and pepper, and toss with the cooked rice, and red and green pepper. Add a pinch of chopped herbs. Make a vinaigrette dressing with 1 tbsp lemon juice, 3 tbsps olive oil and shallot. Toss with the rice. Crush clove of garlic and work it together with the mayonnaise, tomato paste and paprika. Add salt, pepper and the rest of the chopped herbs. Thin with a little milk or hot water. Adjust seasoning. Arrange rice salad on one side of serving dish, and put sole fillets on the other. Spoon mayonnaise dressing over fillets. Divide the two sides with bunches of watercress.

Mussels à la Grecque (top left) and Fin and Feather (left).

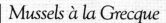

Mussels à la Grecque

PREPARATION TIME: 15 minutes
COOKING TIME: 15 minutes
SERVES: 4 people

2 pints mussels
1 onion, chopped
¼ cup white wine
1½lb tomatoes (or the equivalent in canned tomatoes)
1 clove garlic
Lemon juice
Salt and pepper
Pinch Cayenne pepper
1 chopped shallot
1 tsp fennel seed
1 tsp coriander seeds
1 tsp crushed oregano
1 bay leaf
1 tbsp chopped fresh basil leaves
2 tbsps olive oil

Garnish
Chopped parsley
Black olives

Scrub mussels well, discarding any with broken shells. Put into a pan with chopped onion, white wine, squeeze of lemon juice, salt and pepper. Cover and cook quickly until mussels open, discarding any that do not. Remove mussels from shells and leave to cool. Heat olive oil in a saucepan and add crushed garlic and shallot. Cook until just lightly brown. Blend in the tomatoes, herbs, fennel and coriander seeds. Add seasoning and cooking liquid from the mussels and bring to the boil. Allow the sauce to boil rapidly until well reduced. Leave sauce to cool, then mix with mussels. Serve garnished with chopped parsley and black olives. Serve with green salad and French bread.

Fin and Feather

PREPARATION TIME: 20 minutes
COOKING TIME: 15-20 minutes
OVEN TEMPERATURE: 350°F (180°C)
SERVES: 4 people

4 chicken supremes (boned chicken breasts)
3oz fresh salmon, or canned red salmon
White wine
4 anchovies
⅔ cup olive oil
2 egg yolks
Salt and pepper
1½ tbsps lemon juice
1 tbsp chopped parsley

Garnish
4 small dill pickles
1 tbsp capers
Curly endive

Buy prepared chicken breasts. Put them on a sheet of foil and sprinkle over salt, pepper and a little white wine. Seal foil well. Put into a baking dish and bake in the oven for about 15 minutes, or until cooked through. Open foil packet and allow to cool. Reserve juices from the chicken. Poach the fresh salmon (or drain canned salmon) and remove bones. Put the salmon and anchovies into a food processor bowl or blender and work until broken up. Work in the egg yolks, and salt and pepper. With the machine running, add the oil gradually. Add lemon juice to taste and adjust seasoning. Stir in the cooking liquid from the chicken to give the sauce the consistency of thin cream: if it is too thick add a few drops of milk or water. Put cold chicken breasts onto a plate and coat with all the sauce. Before serving, garnish the dish with capers and pickles. Serve with a green salad or a cold rice salad.

Marinated Herring in Sour Cream with Beet Salad

PREPARATION TIME: 20 minutes
COOKING TIME: 30 minutes
SERVES: 4 people

4 fresh herrings

Marinade
1¼ cups dry white wine
¼ cup white wine vinegar
1 tsp sugar
1 shallot
1 bay leaf
6 black peppercorns
2 sprigs thyme
1 whole clove

Dressing
1¼ cups sour cream or yogurt
½ tsp dry mustard
Salt and pepper

Salad
1 tbsp chopped fennel or dillweed
4 green onions
8 even-sized cooked beets
¼ cup chopped walnuts
2 tbsps red wine vinegar
6 tbsps vegetable oil
Sugar
Salt
Pepper

Fillet the herring, removing heads and tails. Pick out as many of the bones as possible and separate the two fillets of each herring. Put all ingredients for the marinade into a saucepan, bring to the boil and cook for 20 minutes. Pour marinade over herring in a shallow sauté pan. Bring back to the boil and simmer, covered, for about 10 minutes. Leave fish to cool in marinade, then lift out and remove skin. Put herring into a shallow serving dish. Mix sour cream with 2 tbsps of strained marinade, and add mustard, salt and black pepper. Mix until smooth, and pour over fillets. Scatter over the chopped dill and half of the chopped green onions. Peel and slice beets into rounds about ¼" thick, and marinate in the oil, vinegar and sugar. Sprinkle with chopped walnuts and the remaining green onions, and arrange around the marinated herring fillets.

Seafood and Shell Salad

PREPARATION TIME: 20 minutes
COOKING TIME: 25 minutes
SERVES: 4 people

1lb halibut
8oz shrimp
6 Gulf shrimp
¼ pint mussels
1 red pepper
2 tbsps chopped tarragon, or a good pinch of dried tarragon
2 tbsps chopped parsley
4 green onions
Handful of black olives, pitted
8oz pasta shells, cooked
4oz sorrel or fresh spinach
1 bunch watercress
1 tbsp butter
1 tbsp flour
1¼ cups cream, or milk
⅔ cup whipping cream
Salt and pepper

Put halibut into a saucepan and just cover with cold water. Bring to the boil and poach gently till the fish is cooked. Remove pan from heat and allow fish to cool in the liquid. When cool, drain fish, remove all skin and bone, and break flesh into large flakes. Set aside. Scrub mussels. Cook them in their shells with 4 tbsps water or lemon juice. Cover the pan and cook them over the heat quickly until the shells open. Discard any mussels that do not open. Take

mussels out of shells and set aside. Shell all the shrimp. Cook pasta shells until just tender. Rinse under hot, then cold water, and leave to drain dry. Chop red pepper into small cubes, chop the olives and slice the green onions. Mix pasta with peppers, olives, tarragon, parsley and salt and pepper.

Arrange in a large serving dish or small individual dishes, and pile mixed fish and seafood on top. Chill. Cook sorrel or spinach briefly in boiling water. Drain and refresh under cold water. Squeeze dry and chop to a fine purée. Pick over watercress leaves, removing discolored leaves and chopping off

thick ends of stalks with the root hairs. Chop watercress very finely or work in a food processor. Melt butter in a small saucepan over a low heat. Stir in flour and cook over the heat for 2 minutes, stirring all the time. Pour on the milk or cream and stir until well blended. Simmer for about 3 minutes.

This page: Shrimp in Melons (top) and Red Snapper Nicoise (bottom).
Facing page: Seafood and Shell Salad (top) and Seviche (bottom).

Allow sauce to cool slightly, then blend with purée'd sorrel and watercress. Add chopped parsley and tarragon, salt and pepper. Cover top of sauce with a sheet of wax paper to prevent a skin from forming, and allow to cool completely. Whip the cream lightly and fold into the sauce. Pour some of the sauce over the fish, shellfish and pasta. Serve rest of the sauce separately. Garnish with a whole Gulf shrimp if desired.

Red Snapper Niçoise

PREPARATION TIME: 15 minutes

COOKING TIME: 15 minutes

SERVES: 4 people

4 small, whole red snapper
2 tbsps olive oil
Lemon juice
Small can anchovy fillets
½ cup pitted black olives
2 hard-boiled eggs
1 green pepper
1 chopped shallot
1 clove garlic, crushed
½ cup mushrooms
1lb ripe tomatoes
Salt
Pepper
Seasoned flour

Vinaigrette Dressing
2 tbsps red wine vinegar
6 tbsps olive oil
¼ tsp Dijon mustard
Handful of chopped mixed herbs (eg basil, oregano, thyme)

Scale and clean fish, trimming fins but leaving head and tail on. Cut tomatoes into quarters and remove cores. Cut eggs into quarters. Cut olives in half, lengthwise. If mushrooms are small, leave whole; if not, quarter them. Cut green pepper into thin slices, and cut anchovies in half, lengthwise. Prepare vinaigrette dressing and add chopped herbs, garlic and shallot. Put in the mushrooms and leave to marinate in the refrigerator for about 1 hour. Meanwhile, toss fish in seasoned flour to coat lightly. Heat 2 tbsps olive oil in a frying pan and fry fish on both sides until cooked through – about 2-3 minutes per side. When cooking the second side, sprinkle over some lemon juice. Season lightly, and leave to go cold. When ready to serve, add tomatoes, green peppers, eggs and olives to the mushrooms in their marinade, and toss. Pile the salad into a serving dish and arrange the cold, cooked red snapper on top. Garnish with anchovy fillet strips.

Seviche

PREPARATION TIME: 20 minutes

SERVES: 4 people

1lb codfish
⅔ cup lemon or lime juice
1 tbsp chopped shallot
1 green chili pepper
1 green pepper
2 tomatoes
1 tbsp chopped parsley
1 tbsp chopped fresh coriander
2 tbsps vegetable oil
1 small head iceberg lettuce
4 green onions
Salt
Pepper

Skin cod and remove any bones. Wash and pat dry, then cut across grain into slices approximately ½" thick and 2½" long. Put into a bowl and pour over lime or lemon juice. Put in shallot. Slice chili pepper and remove the seeds, then chop finely and add it to the fish. Add seasoning and put into the refrigerator for 24 hours, well covered. Stir occasionally. When ready to serve, chop green onions and herbs. Slice pepper into short, thin strips. Plunge tomatoes into boiling water for about 4 seconds, then into cold water, and peel. Cut tomatoes in half, squeeze out the seeds, and slice into fine strips. Drain off lemon or lime juice from fish, and stir in oil. Add herbs, peppers and tomatoes, and toss. Spoon onto lettuce leaves in a serving dish and sprinkle over spring onions.

Shrimp in Melons

PREPARATION TIME: 25 minutes

SERVES: 4 people

2 small melons
8oz peeled shrimp
Juice of half a lemon
1 small cucumber
4 medium tomatoes
⅓ cup toasted flaked almonds
1 orange
4 tbsps light vegetable oil
¼ cup heavy cream
Salt
Pepper
2 tbsps chopped mint, reserving 4 sprigs for garnish
Pinch of sugar
1 tsp chopped lemon thyme (optional)

Cut melons in half through the middle and scoop out flesh with a melon-baller or spoon, leaving a ¼" border of fruit on the inside of each shell. Cut a thin slice off the bottom of each shell so that they stand upright. Cut the melon into ½" cubes or leave in balls. Peel cucumber, cut in half lengthwise, then into ½" cubes. Peel and squeeze seeds from tomatoes and cut tomatoes into strips. Peel and segment orange. Mix lemon juice, oil and cream together for the dressing. Add chopped mint, and thyme (if desired), a pinch of sugar, and salt and pepper to taste. Toss fruit and vegetables together with the shrimp. Pile ingredients evenly into each melon shell. Chill well and garnish with a small sprig of mint leaves and the almonds.

Lobster and Smoked Chicken Salad

PREPARATION TIME: 25 minutes

SERVES: 4 people

Salad
1 small smoked chicken
1 large cooked lobster
4 sticks celery
4 green onions
4oz pea pods, trimmed
⅓ cup browned cashew nuts
1 head Chinese cabbage
1 head curly endive

Dressing
1¼ cups prepared mayonnaise
2 tbsps soy sauce
1 tsp honey
Sesame seed oil
½ tsp ground ginger
1 tbsp dry sherry, if desired

Garnish
1 red pepper, thinly sliced
2 tbsps chopped parsley

Twist off the claws and legs of lobster. Cut body in half, take out tail meat and set aside. Crack claws and remove meat. Remove as much meat as possible from all the legs. Cut breast meat from the smoked chicken into thin, even slices. Shred the rest of the chicken meat. Mix the shredded chicken and the meat from the lobster claws and legs together. Cut lobster tail meat lengthwise into 3-4 thin slices (depending on size of tail). Set sliced lobster tail and sliced chicken breast aside. Mix celery, cashew nuts and green onions together with the shredded lobster and chicken. Mix the dressing ingredients together – the mayonnaise, soy sauce, sesame oil and honey – and add some black pepper and salt if necessary. Add ground ginger and sherry, if desired. Mix dressing with shredded lobster and chicken. Slice

red pepper into thin strips. Slice Chinese cabbage into thin shreds. Tear curly endive leaves into bite-sized pieces. Pile the greens and pea pods onto a large serving dish. Mound the shredded chicken and lobster salad in the middle. Arrange sliced chicken breast and lobster tail neatly over the top. Garnish with sliced red pepper and chopped parsley. Serve any remaining dressing separately.

Salade aux Fruits de Mer

PREPARATION TIME: 20 minutes

COOKING TIME: 10 minutes

SERVES: 4 people

Salad
8 scallops with roe attached
4oz langoustines, cooked and shelled
4oz shrimp, peeled
½ pint mussels
8oz monkfish
Lemon juice
1 head Romaine lettuce
2 heads Belgian endive (chicory)

Dressing
1 3oz package cream cheese
⅔ cup yogurt
Juice of 1 lemon
3 tbsps milk
1 tbsp Dijon mustard
1 tbsp chopped tarragon
1 tbsp chopped chives
1 tbsp chopped parsley
Salt and pepper

Poach scallops and monkfish in lemon juice and enough water to cover, for about 5 minutes and

leave to cool in the liquid. Scrub mussels well and put into a covered saucepan with 4 tbsps water. Shake pan over heat for about 5 minutes, or until the shells open. Discard mussels whose shells remain closed. Remove mussels from shells and set aside. When scallops and monkfish are cool cut scallops in half, horizontally, and cut monkfish into 1″ pieces. Mix all fish and shellfish together. Remove core from Belgian endive; separate leaves and wash and dry well. Wash Romaine lettuce, remove core and shred finely. To make dressing, blend cheese and milk in a blender or food processor. Add lemon juice, salt and pepper to taste, and mustard, and stir in the chopped herbs. Arrange leaves of Belgian endive onto serving plates. Pile shredded lettuce on top, leaving points of endive leaves showing. Toss shellfish in half the dressing and pile on top of lettuce. Put another spoonful of dressing on top of each serving and serve any remaining dressing separately.

Salade aux Fruits de Mer (above) and Lobster and Smoked Chicken Salad (left).

Main Meals

Pasta and Smoked Salmon

PREPARATION TIME:	10 minutes
COOKING TIME:	18 minutes
SERVES:	4 people

3oz plain tagliatelle or fettuccine
3oz wholemeal tagliatelle or fettuccine
3oz spinach tagliatelle or fettuccine
8oz smoked salmon
¼ cup mushrooms
1 egg
⅔ cup heavy cream
1 tbsp chopped parsley
1 tsp chopped fresh basil
2 green onions, finely chopped
1 tbsp butter
1 jar red salmon caviar
Salt and pepper

Cook the pasta in boiling salted water until just tender. Drain under hot water and keep it warm. Slice and cook the mushrooms, with the onion, in the butter. Slice the smoked salmon into thin strips and set aside. Beat together the egg and heavy cream with the chopped herbs, salt and pepper. Add these to the onion and mushrooms, and heat through, stirring constantly. Do not allow mixture to boil. Toss with the pasta and the salmon. Top with red salmon caviar to serve.

Sole au Vin Rouge

PREPARATION TIME:	15 minutes
COOKING TIME:	25 minutes
OVEN TEMPERATURE:	325°F (160°C)
SERVES:	4 people

2 sole
⅔ cup red wine
¼ cup water
3-4 peppercorns
1 bay leaf
1 slice onion
1 tbsp butter
1 tbsp flour
⅔ cup light cream
1 small bunch purple grapes
Salt
Pepper

Fillet and skin the fish. Wash fillets and dry well, and fold the ends under to make small parcels. Put into an ovenproof dish and pour over the wine and water. Put in the onion slice, peppercorns and bay leaf. Add a pinch of salt, and cover with foil. Put into a pre-set oven and poach for about 10 minutes. Meanwhile, wash and seed the grapes, but leave whole unless very large, in which case halve them. Remove fish from baking dish, cover and keep fillets warm. Heat butter in a small saucepan. When foaming, add flour and cook for

This page: Sole au Vin Rouge (top) and Trout en Papillote (bottom).
Facing page: Pasta and Smoked Salmon (top) and Fritto Misto Mare (bottom).

about 2-3 minutes, until flour is lightly brown. Strain on the cooking liquid from the fish and stir until the sauce comes to the boil. Allow to continue boiling for about 2 minutes. Add cream and re-boil. Season to taste. Arrange fillets in a serving dish. Put the grapes into the sauce to heat them through, reserving a few to garnish. Coat the fish with the sauce to serve.

Spiced Salmon Steaks

PREPARATION TIME: 15 minutes

COOKING TIME: 12-15 minutes

SERVES: 4 people

4 salmon steaks, 1" thick
1 cup light brown sugar
1 tsp ground all-spice
1 tsp dry mustard
1 tsp grated fresh ginger
1 cucumber
1 bunch green onions
2 tsps chopped fresh dill or 1 tsp dry dill weed
1 tbsp chopped parsley
Salt
Pepper
Lemon juice
2 tbsps butter

Mix the sugar and spices together and rub into the surface of both sides of the salmon steaks. Set in a refrigerator for about 1 hour. Peel the cucumber and cut into quarters lengthwise, then remove seeds and cut each quarter into 1" strips. Trim roots of green onions; trim down the green part but leave some green attached. Put these and the cucumber into a saucepan with the butter, lemon juice, salt, pepper, parsley and dill, and cook over a gentle heat for about 10-15 minutes, or until tender. Place salmon steaks under a broiler and cook for about 5-6 minutes on each side. Serve with the cucumber and green onion accompaniment.

Fritto Misto Mare

PREPARATION TIME: 10 minutes

COOKING TIME: 5-6 minutes

SERVES: 4 people

4-8 scallops
8oz uncooked shrimp
1lb whitebait, smelts or sprats, or white fish such as sole or cod
½ pint shelled mussels
Vegetable oil for deep frying
Salt

Batter
1¼ cups water
2 tbsps olive oil
1 cup flour
1 tsp ground nutmeg
1 tsp ground oregano
Pinch salt
1 egg white

Garnish
Parsley sprigs
1 lemon

First make the batter so that it can rest for ½ hour while fish is being prepared. Blend oil with water, and gradually stir it into flour sifted with a pinch of salt. Beat batter until quite smooth, and add the nutmeg and oregano. Just before using, fold in stiffly-beaten egg white. If using smelts or sprats, cut heads off the fish; if using white fish, cut into chunks about 1" thick. Shell shrimp if necessary. If the scallops are large, cut them in half. Heat oil to 375°F (190°C). Dip fish and shellfish, one at a time, into batter, allowing surplus batter to drip off. Then put them into the frying basket and into the hot oil. Fry for 5-6 minutes, or until crisp and golden. Drain on crumpled paper towels. Sprinkle lightly with salt. Put fish on a heated dish. Garnish with parsley sprigs and lemon wedges. If desired, a tartare sauce may be served.

Trout en Papillote

PREPARATION TIME: 15 minutes

COOKING TIME: 10-15 minutes

OVEN TEMPERATURE: 350°F (180°C)

SERVES: 4 people

4 small trout, about 8oz each
2-3 shallots
Sprigs of rosemary
Lemon juice
½ cup butter
¾ cup flaked almonds
Salt
Pepper

Garnish
Slices of lemon

Clean fish well, trim the fins, wash and dry, then season insides. Place a sprig of rosemary inside each, reserving 1 tbsp of leaves for use later. Chop the shallots. Melt the butter. Cut 4 large rounds of foil or baking parchment, brush them with melted butter and place the fish on them. Cut 2-3 slashes on the side of each fish to help them cook quickly. Scatter over the chopped shallots, salt, pepper and some lemon juice, and pour over some of the melted butter. Fold the paper or foil over the fish and seal well. Place fish on a baking sheet and bake for about 10-15 minutes. Meanwhile, brown the almonds in the remaining melted butter and add salt, pepper and a good squeeze of lemon juice. Just before serving, add the reserved rosemary leaves to the hot butter and almonds. Pour over the fish when the parcels are opened, and garnish with lemon slices.

Paella

PREPARATION TIME: 20 minutes

COOKING TIME: 30 minutes

SERVES: 4 people

1lb Gulf shrimp
1 pint mussels in their shells
8oz shrimp in their shells
4oz chorizo (Spanish sausage), sliced
⅔ cup dry white wine
1 cup rice
1 small onion
1 clove garlic, crushed
4 tbsps olive oil
Lemon juice
Saffron
4 tomatoes
2 green peppers
Small bunch green onions, chopped
Salt and pepper

Wash all the shrimp and scrub mussels well, discarding any with broken shells. Cook mussels in the wine over a high heat until the shells open. Discard any that do not open. Strain the liquid for use in cooking the rice. Leave mussels in their shells. Peel half the washed shrimp. Chop the onion finely, heat the oil in a shallow, heatproof dish, and cook the onion and garlic until they become a pale brown. Add the chorizo and cook for 1-2 minutes, then add rice and cook till it looks clear. Add the shellfish liquid, lemon juice, a pinch of saffron and enough water to cover the rice. Cook for 20 minutes on a moderate heat. Remove cores from tomatoes and chop roughly. Slice the peppers and add to the rice during the last 5 minutes of cooking. Add the tomatoes and peeled shrimp to heat through, then add all the remaining shellfish. Adjust seasoning and sprinkle the chopped green onion over to serve.

Paella (left) and Spiced Salmon Steaks (below).

Put tomato sauce and remaining sauce ingredients into a pan and bring to the boil. Turn down the heat and allow to simmer for about 10-15 minutes, then set aside. Bring a large saucepan of salted water to the boil. Trim and wash the pea pods and put them in the boiling water to cook for about 1-2 minutes. Drain and refresh them under cold water. Heat the broiler and brush brochettes with oil. Broil for about 3-5 minutes on each side, basting occasionally with the sauce. Heat some butter in a saucepan and toss the pea pods over the heat with salt and pepper, and heat through. Serve brochettes on their skewers on a bed of cooked rice with almonds, garnished with the lemon wedges and pea pods. Reheat the remaining sauce to serve with the brochettes.

Shrimp Creole with Saffron Rice Ring

PREPARATION TIME: 15 minutes

COOKING TIME: 30 minutes

SERVES: 4 people

1lb shrimp
1 green pepper
1 red pepper
4oz mushrooms
1 medium onion
2 sticks celery
1 16oz can tomatoes
¼ cup butter
1 tsp sugar
1 bay leaf
½ tsp Tabasco
Pinch nutmeg
½ tsp chopped thyme
2 tbsps chopped parsley
1 cup long-grain rice
1 shallot, finely chopped
Good pinch saffron, or 1 pkt saffron powder
Salt
Pepper

Rinse the rice, put into a large saucepan of boiling salted water and cook for about 12 minutes.

Langoustine and Ham Brochettes

PREPARATION TIME: 20 minutes

COOKING TIME: 25 minutes

SERVES: 4 people

16 large raw langoustines or shrimp
8oz ham cut in a thick slice
1 small fresh pineapple
1 green pepper
Oil for basting

Sauce
8oz can tomato sauce
1 tbsp Worcestershire sauce
1 tbsp cider vinegar
1-2 tbsps soft brown sugar
1 clove garlic, crushed
½ tsp dry mustard
1 bay leaf

Garnish
8oz pea pods
2 cups hot, cooked rice, tossed in butter and black pepper
¼ cup toasted flaked almonds

2 tbsps butter
Salt and pepper

Cut most of the fat from the ham. Cut the ham into 1″ cubes. Peel langoustines or shrimp. Halve green pepper, remove the seeds, and cut into 1″ pieces. Peel and quarter the pineapple, remove the core, and cut each quarter into 1″ chunks. Thread a langoustine, pepper, gammon, and pineapple onto each of 4 skewers, continuing until all the ingredients are used.

This page: Shrimp Creole with Saffron Rice Ring.
Facing page: Tuna and Fennel (top) and Langoustine and Ham Brochettes (bottom).

Measure 3 tsps of the boiling water and soak the saffron in it. Melt half the butter and cook the shallot. Butter a 2 cup ring mold well, and set aside. Drain rice when cooked, and mix with cooked shallot, seasoning, 1 tbsp chopped parsley and saffron liquid. Stir well and ensure rice is evenly colored with the saffron. Put this mixture into the ring mold, pressing down well, and leave to keep warm. Melt the remaining butter, chop the onion and celery finely, slice peppers into fine shreds, and slice the mushrooms. Cook the onion in the butter until just lightly colored, then add peppers and mushrooms and cook gently for several minutes. Add celery and tomatoes and bring to the boil. Reduce heat and add the bay leaf, remaining parsley, thyme, Tabasco, sugar and seasoning. Allow to simmer for about 12 minutes, then add shrimp and heat through. Carefully unmold the rice ring onto a serving plate and pour the prawn creole into the center.

Herring and Apples

PREPARATION TIME: 15-20 minutes

COOKING TIME: 50 minutes

OVEN TEMPERATURES: 350°F (180°C) rising to 400°F (200°C)

SERVES: 4 people

4 herrings
1 onion
2 large apples
Dry breadcrumbs
4 large potatoes, peeled and sliced
2/3 cup dry cider or white wine
1 tsp sugar
4 tbsps butter
Salt
Pepper
1 tbsp chopped parsley

Cut heads and tails from herrings, split and bone them, but do not cut into separate fillets. Wash and dry them well. Peel, quarter, core and slice 1 apple. Slice the onion thinly. Butter a shallow baking dish well. Layer the potatoes, apple and onion, seasoning between each layer with salt and pepper, and neatly arranging the final layer of potato slices. Pour the cider or wine over the potatoes, cover the dish with foil and bake for about 40 minutes. Then take the dish from the oven and place herrings on top. Cook, uncovered, for 10 minutes, then sprinkle herrings lightly with breadcrumbs and dot

with some of the butter. Increase heat and bake until herrings brown – about 5-10 minutes. Meanwhile, core remaining apple and slice into rounds, leaving peel on. Melt remaining butter in a saucepan and fry the apples in the butter. Sprinkle them lightly with sugar and continue to fry until a good brown. When herrings have browned, garnish with the apple slices and chopped parsley. Serve in the baking dish.

Tuna and Fennel

PREPARATION TIME: 15 minutes

COOKING TIME: 6-8 minutes

SERVES: 4 people

4 tuna steaks, cut (1") thick
4 tbsps olive oil
4 tbsps white wine
Crushed black pepper
1 clove garlic
Salt
1 head Florentine fennel

Peel garlic and cut into thin slivers. Push these into the tuna steaks with a sharp knife. Mix oil, wine and pepper and pour over steaks in a shallow dish. Leave to marinate in a refrigerator for 1 hour. Heat grill to high and grill fish for 3-4 minutes per side, basting frequently with the marinade. Reserve the green, feathery tops of the fennel. Cut the head in half and slice into 1/4" pieces. Put into boiling salted water and cook for 5 minutes. Season with salt and pepper and keep warm. Garnish the tuna steaks with reserved fennel top and serve with the cooked, sliced fennel.

Buttered Perch

PREPARATION TIME: 10 minutes

COOKING TIME: 12-15 minutes

SERVES: 4 people

2lbs perch (or sole or other whitefish) fillets
1/2 cup butter
3 tbsps oil
Seasoned flour
2 eggs, beaten
Fine corn meal
Lemon juice
Salt

Garnish
Lemon wedges
Parsley sprigs

Skin, wash and dry the fillets well, cut each lengthwise into 4 strips and toss in seasoned flour. Beat the eggs, adding a pinch of salt, then coat the fish before tossing it in the corn meal. Shake off the excess. Heat oil in a large frying pan and add 1 tbsp butter. Shallow-fry the fish briskly for about 5-6 minutes, frying in 2 or 3 batches. Drain on paper towels and keep warm. Melt remaining butter and add lemon juice. Pour over the fish and serve with lemon wedges and sprigs of parsley.

Hazelnut Flounder

PREPARATION TIME: 15 minutes

COOKING TIME: 10 minutes

SERVES: 4 people

2 large flounder, filleted (sole or
   whitefish may be used)
2 eggs, lightly beaten, with a pinch of
   salt
½ cup dry breadcrumbs
½ cup ground browned hazelnuts
2 tbsps oil
4 tbsps butter
Salt
Pepper
Flour

Garnish
1 large bunch watercress
⅓ cup hazelnuts, crushed
Lemon wedges

**Buttered Perch (left) and
Herring and Apples (below).**

Fillet the fish and coat lightly in flour. Dip fillets into the beaten eggs, then into a mixture of the crumbs and nuts. Sauté the fillets quickly in oil until browned on both sides. Add salt and pepper to taste. Remove fillets from pan and keep warm. Wipe out the pan and melt the butter in it. Add crushed hazelnuts to the butter and fry them until they are a nice golden brown. Serve the fillets with the hazelnuts on top, garnished with lemon wedges and a bunch of watercress.

Stuffed Salmon Trout

PREPARATION TIME: 10-15 minutes

COOKING TIME: 40-60 minutes

OVEN TEMPERATURE: 350°F (180°C)

SERVES: 4 people

1 fresh whole salmon trout weighing 2-2½lbs
1 head Florentine fennel
2lbs fresh spinach
¼ cup walnuts
1 shallot, chopped
1 cup fresh white breadcrumbs
1 tbsp chopped parsley
1 tbsp chopped thyme
4 tbsps butter, melted
Juice of 2 lemons
Grated nutmeg
Salt
Pepper

Garnish
Lemon slices

Have the fish boned for stuffing. The head and tail should be left on. Sprinkle the inside with some of the butter and all but 2 tbsps of the lemon juice. Place fish in the center of a large, lightly buttered square of foil, and set aside. Prepare the stuffing. Cut the head of fennel in half (or, if large, into quarters), then into ¼" slices, and put in a pan of boiling water to cook for 2-3 minutes. Meanwhile, wash the spinach leaves well, and tear off any coarse stalks. Put into a large pan, sprinkled with salt. Cover and cook for about 3 minutes, then drain and chop finely. Chop the

shallot finely and soften in 1 tbsp of the remaining melted butter. Add to the spinach with the fennel slices, chopped walnuts, parsley, thyme, nutmeg, salt and pepper, 1 tbsp of the lemon juice, and the breadcrumbs. Fill the salmon with the stuffing, leaving a border of stuffing showing. Seal the foil over the top of the fish to enclose it, but do not wrap too tightly. Place in a roasting pan and bake for 40-60 minutes, depending on weight. To serve, unwrap and transfer to a large serving dish. Remove skin from one side, turn over carefully and remove skin from the other. Serve with remaining melted butter sharpened with remaining lemon juice, and garnish with sliced lemon.

Hazelnut Flounder (left), Salmon with Cucumber Cream (below) and Stuffed Salmon Trout (facing page).

Coulibiac

PREPARATION TIME: 30 minutes
COOKING TIME: 35-40 minutes
OVEN TEMPERATURE:
400°F (200°C)
SERVES: 4 people

Pastry
4 cups all-purpose flour
4 sticks butter
Salt
⅔ cup iced water
1 egg, beaten

Filling
1lb fresh salmon
4 small leeks
⅓ cup rice
2 hard-boiled eggs
4 tbsps butter or margarine
8oz mushrooms
2 tbsps chopped parsley
1 tbsp chopped thyme
Salt
Pepper

Sauce
1¼ cups sour cream
¼ tsp grated horseradish
1 small bunch chives
Salt and pepper

Skin, trim and bone the salmon, and cut into 4 equal-sized pieces. Cook rice until tender, rinse under hot water and set aside to cool. Slice mushrooms and clean leeks well, trimming their root ends. Cut leeks into lengths equal to those of the salmon, put them into a saucepan of cold water and bring to the boil. Cook until almost completely tender, drain and allow to cool. Cook mushrooms for a few minutes in the butter. Add rice, parsley, thyme and seasoning. Hard boil the eggs for about 10 minutes and leave to sit in cold water. To prepare the pastry, cut the butter into ½″ cubes. Sieve flour with a pinch of salt into a bowl and add cubed butter until it is well coated. Mix in the iced water, a little at a time, until the mixture just holds together. (The full quantity of water may not be needed.) Chill mixture for about 10 minutes in the refrigerator. Turn the dough out onto a well-floured surface and shape it into a rough square. Using a well-floured rolling pin, roll out to a rectangle 3 times as long as it is wide. Fold the bottom third of the dough up to the middle and the top third over it. Give the dough a half-turn, then roll out and fold again in the same way. Repeat the process once more, chilling the dough in between operations if the pastry gets too soft. Chill before using. Roll out the pastry to a square ¼″ thick and cut into 4 even-sized pieces approximately 6″ square. Save the trimmings. Brush each square with water and put a layer of the rice and mushroom mixture onto each. Place the cut pieces of leek on top of the rice, then put on another layer of rice. Cut the hard-boiled eggs in half and put one half on the rice layer. Add another layer of rice and, finally, the salmon piece. Fold the pastry over the salmon like an envelope and seal the edges well. Turn the envelope over and put onto a lightly-greased baking sheet. Brush each parcel with lightly beaten egg and cut the pastry trimmings into shapes to decorate the top. Brush these decorations with egg. Make a small hole in the center of each parcel. Bake until pastry is brown and salmon has had time to cook – about 30 minutes. Meanwhile, prepare a sour cream sauce. Chop the chives and mix with the sour cream, horseradish and seasoning. Keep the sauce at room temperature, but just before serving heat it over a gentle heat. Do not allow to boil. Serve the sauce with the coulibiac and garnish with watercress if desired.

This page: Coulibiac (top) and Broiled Cod Steaks (bottom). Facing page: Sea Bass with Vegetables.

Broiled Cod Steaks

PREPARATION TIME: 10 minutes
COOKING TIME: 9 minutes
SERVES: 4 people

4 cod steaks, each about 1″ thick
3 tbsps butter
Dry breadcrumbs
Pepper

Flavored Butters

½ cup unsalted butter
1 tbsp chopped parsley and 1 tbsp
    chopped thyme,
or 1 clove crushed garlic,
or 2 tsps anchovy paste, or 2 tsps
    tomato paste and 1 tbsp chopped
    chives and a few drops of Tabasco
Salt and pepper

Garnish
4 ripe tomatoes

Melt the 3 tbsps butter. Pre-heat broiler. Brush both sides of the cod steaks with some of the melted butter. Wash tomatoes, dry them well and cut them in half. Broil with the cod steaks for about 3 minutes. Turn the steaks, brush with more melted butter, and season with pepper. Dust with dry breadcrumbs. Broil for a further 6 minutes, basting well with the butter. To serve, top each steak with a slice of one of the flavored butters and the broiled tomato halves.

To prepare flavored butters, cream the unsalted butter until soft. Beat in either the herbs, or garlic, or anchovy paste, or tomato paste, chives and Tabasco. Add seasoning to taste and a squeeze of lemon juice if desired. When well mixed, pile onto a sheet of plastic wrap or wax paper and twist ends to shape the butter into a cylinder. Chill in the refrigerator until firm. The butter may also be frozen.

Broiled Red Snapper with Garlic Sauce

PREPARATION TIME: 15 minutes

COOKING TIME: 8-10 minutes

SERVES: 4 people

4 small red snapper
Olive oil
Lemon juice
Pepper

Garlic Sauce
2 egg yolks
½ tsp mustard powder
1¼ cups olive oil
2 tbsps lemon juice
1 or 2 cloves crushed garlic
Salt
White pepper

Garnish
Lemon wedges
Watercress

Put egg yolks, mustard, garlic, salt and pepper into a food processor or blender (an electric mixer can also be used). Beat ingredients together until yolks thicken slightly. Begin adding oil in a thin, steady stream while beating yolks. Be sure to use all the oil. When sauce has thickened, adjust seasoning, add lemon and set aside. Scale and clean the fish well, leaving heads and tails on. Cut 2-3 slashes on both sides of each fish, brush with oil, and sprinkle with pepper and some lemon juice. Put under a broiler for 4-5 minutes each side. Serve with lemon wedges and the garlic sauce. Garnish with watercress if desired.

Turbot in Lettuce Leaves

PREPARATION TIME: 15 minutes

COOKING TIME: 18 minutes

OVEN TEMPERATURE:
350°F (180°C)

SERVES: 4 people

2lbs turbot fillets
1 large Romaine lettuce
1 chopped shallot
⅔ cup dry Italian vermouth
⅔ cup heavy cream
4 tbsps butter
2 tbsps flour
1 tbsp chopped chervil or parsley
Salt and pepper
Lemon juice

Skin and wash the turbot fillets well. Trim into even-sized pieces. Trim and separate the lettuce leaves. Keep them whole and put the largest, best-looking ones into boiling water for less than 1 minute. Remove them with a slotted spoon, refresh in cold water and leave to drain. Cut remaining lettuce into thin strips and put into boiling water. Drain almost immediately and refresh them. Season the fillets and place on the whole lettuce leaves, hiding the fish trimmings underneath. Wrap the leaves securely round the fillets. Butter a large ovenproof dish and put in the wrapped fillets, folded side down. Pour over the wine. Sprinkle over the chopped shallot and poach for about 10-12 minutes. When cooked, take fillets out of the baking dish, leave them in their lettuce leaves and keep warm. Melt remaining butter in a saucepan and, when foaming, stir in the flour. Cook for 2-3 minutes or until flour is pale brown. Strain in the cooking liquid from the fish, stir well and bring to the boil. When sauce thickens, add cream and re-boil. Add the blanched lettuce shreds, adjust seasoning and add lemon juice if necessary. Stir in the chopped chervil or parsley just before serving and pour the sauce into the serving dish. Set the fish parcels on top of the sauce to serve.

Sea Bass with Vegetables

PREPARATION TIME: 30 minutes

COOKING TIME: 40-60 minutes

OVEN TEMPERATURE:
350°F (180°C)

SERVES: 4 people

1 sea bass, weighing 2-2½lbs
8oz broccoli or green beans
1lb new potatoes
4 zucchini
4 very small turnips
1 small bunch green onions
2 carrots
4 tbsps butter
2 tbsps flour
1¼ cups milk
1 small bunch fresh thyme
3 lemons
Paprika
Chopped parsley
Salt and pepper

Clean the bass, trim the fins, but leave the head and tail on. Put seasoning and thyme inside the fish. Put the fish in the center of a large square of buttered foil. Add the juice of 1 lemon, wrap fish loosely, and bake for 40-60 minutes, depending on weight. Cut broccoli into small flowerets (or trim beans, but leave whole). Scrub potatoes and turnips but do not peel. Trim ends of zucchini and cut into 2" strips. Trim roots and tops from the green onions, leaving on some of the green. Peel carrots, and cut to same size as zucchini. Keeping the vegetables in separate piles, steam potatoes and turnips for 15-20 minutes, the carrots, broccoli or beans for 6 minutes, and the zucchini and green onions for 3 minutes. Arrange on a serving dish and keep warm.

Remove fish from wrapping and place in the middle of the vegetables, keep them warm while preparing the sauce. Melt the butter and cook the flour in it for 1-2 minutes until pale brown. Stir in the milk and allow sauce to boil for 1-2 minutes until thick. Strain in the cooking liquid from the fish. Peel and segment remaining lemons, working over a bowl to collect any juice. Chop the thyme and add to sauce along with lemon segments and juice. Sprinkle paprika on the potatoes, and chopped parsley on the carrots. Coat the fish with the lemon sauce and serve.

Salmon with Cucumber Cream

PREPARATION TIME: 15 minutes

COOKING TIME: 20 minutes

OVEN TEMPERATURE:
350°F (180°C)

SERVES: 4 people

4 salmon cutlets (tail pieces)
2 tbsps butter
1 small cucumber
2 tbsps light stock
⅔ cup milk
2 tbsps flour
Salt
Pepper
Lemon juice
Pinch sugar
Nutmeg
¼ cup heavy cream

Grate cucumber. Melt the butter in a saucepan, add half the cucumber and cook slowly for about 10 minutes. Add flour and stir to blend. Stir in the stock and milk, bring to boil, then allow to cook slowly until cucumber has softened. Put the contents of the

pan into a blender or food processor and purée with the lemon juice, sugar, nutmeg, salt and pepper until smooth. Stir in remaining cucumber. Pour the cream over the top of the hot sauce and set aside in a saucepan while cooking the fish. Skin the cutlets and put into a baking dish with water and seasoning. Poach for 10 minutes, then remove from oven and keep warm. Re-heat cucumber sauce, stir in the cream and allow to boil for 1 minute. Spoon some of the sauce onto serving plates and put the salmon cutlets on top. Coat with more of the sauce.

Broiled Red Snapper with Garlic Sauce (left) and Turbot in Lettuce Leaves (below).

Lobster Newburg

PREPARATION TIME: 10 minutes	
COOKING TIME: 12 minutes	
SERVES: 4 people	

1 large cooked lobster
1¼ cups heavy cream
2 egg yolks
2 tbsps butter
¼ cup dry sherry
Salt
Pepper
¼ tsp paprika
Cayenne pepper
1 tsp tomato paste

Heat the butter in a medium saucepan, add paprika and cook for 1 minute. Cut lobster in half. Take off tail and claws, remove the meat from these sections. Remove as much meat from the rest of the lobster as possible, add it to the pan, along with tail and claw meat. Put in the sherry and cook for 1 minute. Remove the tail and claw meat, and set aside for garnish. Mix egg yolks and cream together, and put in the pan with the lobster. Add the paprika, Cayenne, tomato paste and seasoning, and cook over a very low heat until the mixture begins to thicken. Serve with buttered rice, tossed with parsley. Garnish with the tail and claw meat.

Broiled Swordfish Steaks with Grapefruit

PREPARATION TIME: 10 minutes	
COOKING TIME: 10 minutes	
SERVES: 4 people	

4 swordfish steaks, 1" thick
4 tbsps melted butter (or 4 tbsps oil)
2 grapefruit
1 tbsp sugar
Coarsely ground pepper

Melt butter, and brush fish steaks on both sides. Heat broiler to moderate. Season steaks with coarsely ground pepper. Broil on one side for about 5 minutes, turn, brush again with butter, then broil for about 3 minutes. Slice one grapefruit thinly, and peel and segment the other. Sprinkle the slices with sugar and brown under the broiler. Put the segments on top of the fish and heat through for 1 minute. Overlap the broiled grapefruit slices on serving plates and put the fish on top.

Shrimp Florentine

PREPARATION TIME: 15 minutes	
COOKING TIME: 15-20 minutes	
SERVES: 4 people	

1lb cooked shrimp
2lbs fresh spinach
1 cup mushrooms
2 tomatoes, seeds removed
1 shallot
4 tbsps butter
1 tbsp flour
1¼ cups milk
½ cup grated Cheddar cheese
½ tsp Dijon mustard
Salt
Pepper
Nutmeg

Rinse spinach well, removing any thick stalks, and put it into a saucepan with a good pinch of salt. Cover and cook for about 3-5 minutes. In a small saucepan, heat half of the butter. Chop the shallot finely and cook it in the butter until soft. Wipe and slice the mushrooms and cook with the

This page: Shrimp Florentine (top) and Broiled Swordfish Steaks with Grapefruit (bottom).
Facing page: Lobster Newburg (top) and Skate with Capers, Olives and Shallots (bottom).

shallots. Drain the spinach well and chop finely. Mix the shallots, mushrooms and tomatoes with the spinach, add seasoning and a pinch of nutmeg, and put into an ovenproof dish. Melt half the remaining butter in a saucepan and

add the flour. Gradually stir in the milk, return the sauce to the heat and bring to the boil. Season with salt and pepper, and add mustard. Grate the cheese and add half to the sauce. Shell shrimp if necessary. Heat remaining butter and quickly toss shrimp in it over heat. Put shrimp on top of the spinach and cover with sauce. Sprinkle remaining cheese over, and brown quickly under a broiler. Serve immediately.

Skate with Capers, Olives and Shallots

PREPARATION TIME: 10 minutes

COOKING TIME: 15 minutes

OVEN TEMPERATURE: 350°F (180°C)

SERVES: 4 people

4 wings of skate
2 tbsps capers
2 shallots, chopped
½ cup stoned black olives, sliced
½ cup butter
1 tbsp chopped mixed herbs
1¼ cups white wine and water mixed
1 bay leaf
4 peppercorns
Salt
Lemon juice

Put the skate into a baking dish with the wine, water, bay leaf, salt and peppercorns. Cover and poach in the oven for 10 minutes. Drain well, removing any skin, and keep warm. Melt the butter and cook the shallots quickly, to brown both. Add capers and olives to heat through. Add herbs and lemon juice. Pour over the skate and serve immediately.

Monkfish Piperade

PREPARATION TIME: 20 minutes

COOKING TIME: 30 minutes

OVEN TEMPERATURE: 350°F (180°C)

SERVES: 4 people

1½lbs monkfish fillets
2 onions
1 yellow pepper
1 red pepper
1 green pepper
1-2 cloves garlic
1 8oz can tomatoes
Salt
Pepper
2-3 tbsps olive oil
1 small loaf French bread
Oil for deep frying

Slice onions thinly and soften in 1 tbsp olive oil in a saucepan. Slice all the peppers in half, remove seeds, and cut into ½" strips. Crush garlic and add to onions when tender, then cook gently for another 5 minutes. Add tomatoes and seasoning and let sauce simmer until liquid has reduced by about half. If the fish fillets are large, cut them in half again lengthwise. Heat remaining oil in a saucepan and cook the fish until it is lightly brown. Transfer fish to an ovenproof dish, and when the piperade is ready, spoon it over the top of the fillets, and heat through in the oven for about 10 minutes. Meanwhile, slice the French bread on the slant into ½" slices. Fry in enough oil to barely cover until golden brown, then drain on paper towels. Put the monkfish piperade into a serving dish and surround with the bread.

Halibut and Crab Hollandaise

PREPARATION TIME: 15 minutes

COOKING TIME: 20 minutes

OVEN TEMPERATURE: 325°F (160°C)

SERVES: 4 people

4 large fillets of halibut
¼ cup white wine
1 bay leaf
Slice of onion
8oz crabmeat
2 tbsps heavy cream
1 tbsp butter
1 tbsp flour
3 egg yolks
½ cup butter, melted
1 tbsp lemon juice
Salt and pepper
Cayenne pepper
Paprika

Poach the fish with the bay leaf, onion slice, wine and just enough water to cover. Cover the baking dish and cook for about 10 minutes in the oven. Put egg yolks, lemon juice, Cayenne and paprika into a blender or food processor. Turn on the machine, and gradually pour the melted butter through the feed tube. When the sauce has thickened, set it aside. Remove fish from baking dish, cover and keep warm. Put the remaining butter in a saucepan and add the flour, stirring well. Strain on the cooking liquid from the fish, stir well and bring to the boil. Add cream and bring back to the boil for 2-3 minutes. Adjust the seasoning of the sauce, mix it

with the crab meat, and put into the bottom of an ovenproof dish that can also be used for serving. Put the fish on top of the crab meat and coat over with the Hollandaise sauce. Quickly brown the sauce under a broiler before serving.

Danish Sole and Shrimp

PREPARATION TIME: 15 minutes

COOKING TIME: 10-15 minutes

SERVES: 4 people

2 large sole
8oz shrimp
Seasoned flour
6 tbsps butter
2 tbsps oil
Salt
Pepper
Lemon juice

Garnish
Lemon wedges

Peel the tails, shells and legs from 4 whole shrimp and set aside. Fillet and skin the sole, rinse and dry well, and coat lightly in seasoned flour. Heat the oil in a large frying pan, then drop in 2 tbsps of the butter. Lay in the fish fillets and cook quickly to brown both sides. Transfer them to a serving dish and keep warm. Briefly cook the remaining peeled shrimp in the butter remaining in the pan and scatter them over the cooked fillets. Wipe out the pan, put in the remaining butter, and cook to a good nut brown colour. Add a squeeze of lemon juice. Adjust seasoning, then pour over the sole and shrimp. Garnish with the whole shrimp and lemon wedges.

Rock Salmon in Paprika Sauce

PREPARATION TIME: 20 minutes

COOKING TIME: 16 minutes

OVEN TEMPERATURE: 350°F (180°C)

SERVES: 4 people

1lb rock salmon fillets (other white fish may be substituted)
Lemon juice
Bay leaf
Slice of onion
6 peppercorns
2 tbsps butter
2 tbsps flour
¼ cup mushrooms
1 small red pepper

1¼ cups milk
2 tsps sweet paprika pepper
1 clove garlic, crushed
1 chopped shallot
1 tbsp chopped parsley
1 tsp chopped thyme
1 tsp tomato paste
8oz freshly cooked pasta
2 tbsps sour cream or yogurt
Salt
Pepper

Cut the fillets into 1" chunks. Put into an ovenproof dish with water to cover, lemon juice, bay leaf,

onion slice and peppercorns. Cover and poach for about 10 minutes. Slice mushrooms finely. Slice the red pepper in half, core and seed it, then slice into thin shreds. Melt the butter in a saucepan, add mushrooms and shallot and cook for about 1 minute. Add garlic, red peppers, and sweet paprika pepper and allow to cook for about 2-3 minutes. Add the flour. Stir in well, and pour on the milk and the poaching liquid from the fish. Bring the sauce to the boil and allow to cook for 2-3 minutes and add thyme, parsley and tomato paste. Add salt and pepper to taste. Arrange the freshly cooked pasta in a serving dish and place the chunks of fish on top of the pasta. Coat over with paprika sauce and spoon over the yogurt or sour cream to serve.

Danish and Monkfish Piperade (below).

Mackerel with Herb-Mustard Butter

PREPARATION TIME: 15 minutes	
COOKING TIME: 12-20 minutes	
SERVES: 4 people	

4 mackerel
6 tbsps whole grain mustard
1 tbsp chopped parsley
1 tbsp snipped chives
1 tbsp chopped lemon thyme
1 tbsp chopped fresh basil
1 cup butter
Salt
Pepper
Lemon juice

Garnish
1 bunch watercress

Wash and trim the mackerel, leaving heads and tails on. Cut 3 slashes on each side and spread 1 tbsp mustard over each fish. Sprinkle with freshly ground pepper. Melt the butter and sprinkle about 1 tsp over each fish. Grill them for 6-10 minutes on each side, depending on their size. Mix remaining butter and mustard with the herbs, seasoning and lemon juice. When fish are cooked put them into a serving dish and pour over the herb-mustard butter. Garnish with the watercress.

Sardine and Tomato Gratinée

PREPARATION TIME: 20-25 minutes	
COOKING TIME: 15 minutes	
OVEN TEMPERATURE: 425°F (225°C)	
SERVES: 4 people	

2lbs large, fresh sardines
3 tbsps olive oil
⅔ cup dry white wine
8oz tomatoes
4 anchovies
2 tbsps dry breadcrumbs
¼ cup grated Parmesan cheese
2 tbsps chopped fresh herbs
2 leeks, cleaned and sliced
Salt and pepper

Scale and clean the sardines. Heat oil in a large frying pan, add the sardines and brown well on both sides. Remove from the pan and set aside. Add leeks and cook slowly in the oil from the sardines. When they are soft, pour in the wine and boil to reduce by about two-thirds. Add tomatoes, salt pepper and herbs, and continue to simmer for 1 minute. Pour into an ovenproof dish and put the sardines on top. Sprinkle with the cheese and breadcrumbs. Bake for about 5 minutes. If desired, cut anchovy fillets lengthwise into thinner strips and lay them on top of the gratinée before serving.

This page: Halibut and Crab Hollandaise (top) and Sardine and Tomato Gratinée (bottom). Facing page: Rock Salmon in Paprika Sauce (top) and Mackerel with Herb-Mustard Butter.

Snacks and Savories

Strawberry Shrimp

PREPARATION TIME: 10 minutes

COOKING TIME: 3 minutes

SERVES: 4 people

¾lb shrimp, shelled and minced
1 small can water chestnuts, peeled
    and minced
½ cup ham, ground
1 tsp white wine
¼ tsp minced green onion
¼ tsp grated fresh ginger
1½ tbsps cornstarch
1 egg white
Sesame seeds
Pinch of salt
Oil for deep frying
4 tbsps hoisin (Chinese barbecue)
    sauce
1 tsp white or rice wine vinegar
1 tsp honey
2 tbsps water
1 tsp sesame oil

Mix prawns and water chestnuts
with wine, green onion, ginger, egg
white and a pinch of salt. Chill
mixture for 30 minutes before
using. Form mixture into
strawberry-sized balls. Cover each
ball with the finely ground ham.
Fry in deep oil for about 3 minutes
at 375°F (190°C). Drain, roll in
sesame seeds to coat, and place on
a plate. Mix hoisin sauce, honey,
vinegar, water and sesame oil
together, and serve with the shrimp
balls. Garnish shrimp balls with
parsley.

Fisherman's Pie

PREPARATION TIME: 20 minutes

COOKING TIME: 45 minutes

OVEN TEMPERATURE:
375°F (190°C)

SERVES: 4 people

1lb cod fillet
1lb smoked cod or haddock fillet
¼ pint clams
4oz peeled shrimp
1¼ cups milk
½ cup water
1 bay leaf
2 tbsps butter
2 tbsps flour
1 heaped tbsp chopped parsley

Squeeze of lemon juice
Salt
Freshly ground pepper

Topping
1½ lbs potatoes
1-2 tbsps milk
2 tbsps butter
Salt
Pepper

Skin fish and cut into pieces. Keep
fresh cod and smoked fish separate.
Put each into a separate saucepan
with milk, water, and half a bay leaf
in each. Bring to the boil; lower
heat, and simmer, covered, for
about 10 minutes. Meanwhile, peel
potatoes and cut them into even-
sized chunks. Add them to a pan of
cold, salted water, bring up to the
boil and cook for about 20
minutes, or until tender. Drain,
return to the hot saucepan and
shake over heat until they are dry.
Mash them, and beat in 2 or 3
tbsps hot milk and half the butter.
Season with salt and pepper and
set aside. Take cooked fish from the
milk and break it up, removing any
bones. Strain cooking liquid from
both saucepans – there should be

**This page: Kedgeree.
Facing page: Strawberry
Shrimp (top) and Crab Toasts
(bottom).**

1¼ cups in all. Melt butter in a
saucepan over a low heat. Stir in
the flour, and cook gently for 1
minute. Gradually stir in the
reserved fish liquid. Bring to boil.
Stir well and simmer for 2-3
minutes. Take off the heat. Fold in

the fish and parsley, and add lemon juice, a seasoning of salt and pepper, clams and shrimp. Butter a 2½ cup ovenproof dish and put the fish mixture in it. Fill a pastry bag, fitted with a rosette tube, with the mashed potato mixture and pipe in a lattice over the surface of the fish. Pipe a border round its edge. Dot over the remaining butter in pieces, and put into the oven for about 20 minutes and brown under a broiler, with grated cheese sprinkled on top if desired.

Crab Ramekins

PREPARATION TIME: 10 minutes
COOKING TIME: 15 minutes
OVEN TEMPERATURE: 425°F (220°C)
SERVES: 4 people

¾ cup Cheddar cheese
¾ cup Parmesan cheese
1½ cups fresh white breadcrumbs
1¼ cups cream
1 cup crabmeat
3 eggs
1 tsp Worcestershire sauce
Cayenne pepper
Ground mace
Dry mustard
Salt and pepper

Separate the eggs and grate the cheese. Mix the breadcrumbs with the cream and grated cheese. Add the Worcestershire sauce, a pinch of mace, Cayenne, dry mustard and seasoning. Beat in the egg yolks. Whip the whites until stiff but not dry and fold into the cheese mixture along with the crabmeat. Pour into a large, buttered, ovenproof dish or smaller ramekin dishes. Bake until risen.

Smoked Haddock Lyonnaise

PREPARATION TIME: 15 minutes
COOKING TIME: 20 minutes
SERVES: 4 people

3 medium onions
1 tbsp unsalted butter
2 tbsps oil
3 medium-sized potatoes
1lb smoked haddock (finnan haddie)
Freshly ground pepper
2 tbsps white wine vinegar
Chopped parsley

Heat oil in a large frying pan and, when hot, drop in butter. Cut

smoked fish into chunks and sauté. Remove from the pan and set aside. Slice onions and cook them slowly in the butter until they turn golden brown. Slice the potatoes and cook in boiling salted water until slightly softened. Add them just as onions are turning color, then sauté the mixture to brown lightly. Add the smoked fish, sauté for a few minutes, and adjust seasoning. Pile onto a serving platter. Add vinegar to the pan, bring rapidly to boil, add chopped parsley, and pour over potatoes and haddock.

Crab and Spinach Roulade

PREPARATION TIME: 15 minutes
COOKING TIME: 18 minutes
OVEN TEMPERATURE: 400°F (200°C)
SERVES: 4 people

Roulade
1lb spinach, washed
1 tbsp butter
4 eggs, separated

Parmesan cheese, grated
Salt
Pepper

Filling
½ cup crabmeat
¼ cup mushrooms, thinly sliced
1 tbsp butter
1 tbsp flour
⅔ cup milk
Nutmeg
2-3 tbsps cream
Paprika
Cayenne pepper
Lemon juice

Cook the spinach in boiling salted water for about 5 minutes. Drain, rinse under cold water, and press well to remove excess liquid. Put the spinach into a food processor with the butter and egg yolks and process to a smooth purée. Whisk egg whites until they are stiff but not dry and fold into the spinach mixture. Line a 12″ x 8″ jelly roll pan with wax paper. Spread in the spinach mixture very quickly and dust lightly with Parmesan cheese. Bake in the top half of the oven for about 10 minutes or until mixture has risen and is firm to the touch. Meanwhile, prepare filling. Sauté sliced mushrooms in butter. Remove from heat, and add flour, paprika, Cayenne, lemon juice and

seasoning to taste. Pour on the milk and bring to the boil, then simmer to a creamy consistency. Draw pan from heat and stir in nutmeg and cream (a dash of Tabasco and 1 tbsp dry sherry can also be used if desired). Once the pan is again off the heat, stir in the crabmeat. When the roulade is cooked, quickly turn it out onto a clean towel, cheese side down, and peel off the paper in which it was cooked. Spread it with the filling, roll up as for a jelly roll, starting at the short end, and serve sprinkled with more Parmesan cheese if desired.

Crab Toasts

PREPARATION TIME: 10 minutes
COOKING TIME: 4 minutes per piece
SERVES: 4 people

8 slices white bread
8oz crabmeat
3 tbsps minced water chestnuts
1 egg white
½ tsp white wine
½ tsp mustard powder
½ tsp salt
½ tsp minced green onion
¼ tsp grated ginger
1½ tsps cornstarch
1 tbsp minced parsley
Oil for deep frying

Remove crusts from the bread, and slice diagonally across each piece to form 2 triangles. Mix crabmeat and chestnuts together. Add egg white, wine, salt, green onion, ginger and cornstarch. Heap the mixture generously onto each triangle of bread. Sprinkle with parsley, pressing down firmly so that the mixture will not float off during frying. Heat oil to 350°F (180°C). Put a piece of the prepared bread, crabmeat side down, onto a slotted spoon, place it in the oil and gently remove spoon. Fry the pieces, a few at a time, until the bread side becomes a golden brown. Turn each piece over and fry again. Drain on paper towels and keep warm in the oven until all the pieces are finished.

Crab Ramekins (above right) and Smoked Haddock Lyonnaise (right) and Fisherman's Pie (inset above).

Oysters and Apples

PREPARATION TIME: 10 minutes	
COOKING TIME: 2-3 minutes	
SERVES: 4 people	

1 3½oz can smoked oysters
1 large apple, unpeeled
4-5 strips bacon
1oz Cheddar cheese

Core and quarter the apple, and cut the quarters into 8-10 slices. Divide the cheese into 8-10 small pieces. Put 1 piece on each slice of apple and an oyster on top of the cheese. Cut each bacon strip in half. Wrap the bacon around the oysters and apples. Secure with a wooden pick and broil until the bacon is crisp, turning once.

Shrimp Pastry Puffs

PREPARATION TIME: 15 minutes	
COOKING TIME: 25-30 minutes	
OVEN TEMPERATURE: 400°F (200°C)	
SERVES: 4 people	

Choux Pastry
½ cup flour
⅓ cup butter
½ cup water
2-3 eggs
Salt

Filling
1¼ cups milk
2½ tbsps butter
2½ tbsps flour
2 tbsps white wine
¾ cup shrimp
2 hard-boiled eggs, quartered
Nutmeg
1 bay leaf
1 tsp chopped dill
Salt
Pepper

Prepare the pastry. Sift flour with a pinch of salt. Place butter and water in a pan over a gentle heat. When butter is melted, bring water to the boil. Take off the heat and immediately tip in all the flour. Beat until the mixture is smooth and leaves the sides of the pan. Leave to cool. Whisk the eggs lightly and add by degrees to the mixture, beating thoroughly between each addition. (This part of the recipe may be done with an electric mixer or in a food processor). When finished, the paste should be

smooth and shiny and hold its shape when dropped from a spoon. Lightly grease a baking sheet and sprinkle it lightly with water. Place the pastry mixture by heaped teaspoonfuls onto the sheet. If desired, the puffs can be made slightly larger by using a tablespoon. Bake until the puffs are firm to the touch and a good golden brown. For the sauce, melt

the butter over a gentle heat and blend in the flour. Stir in the milk gradually and add the bay leaf. Add the wine and bring the mixture to the boil, stirring constantly. Remove the bay leaf, add the shrimp, dill and eggs, and adjust the seasoning. Cut the pastry puffs almost in half through the middle and fill with the shrimp and egg mixture. Serve hot or cold.

This page: Crab and Spinach Roulade (top) and Shrimp Risotto (bottom).
Facing page: Shrimp Pastry Puffs (top) and Oysters and Apples (bottom).

shell fish, anchovies, olives and capers. Place cheese slices on top of the fish. Bake in a pre-set oven until cheese browns lightly and the crust is crisp.

Anchovy Pâté with Crudités

PREPARATION TIME:	15 minutes
SERVES:	4 people

8oz canned anchovies
¼ cup olive oil
1 3 oz package cream cheese
½ cup pitted black olives
2 tbsps capers
1 tbsp Dijon mustard
1 tsp ground pepper

Put all ingredients into the bowl of a blender or food processor and run the machine until well mixed. The mixture may have to be worked in 2 batches. Serve with French bread or toast, and raw vegetables of all kinds – tomatoes, mushrooms, celery, radishes, green beans, cauliflower, carrots, cucumber, peppers, spring onions, or quarters of hard boiled eggs.

Goujons

PREPARATION TIME:	20-30 minutes
COOKING TIME:	2-3 minutes
SERVES:	4 people

2 sole
Seasoned flour
1 egg
2 tsps olive oil
Dry breadcrumbs
Oil for deep frying
Pinch of salt

Tartare Sauce
2 tbsps mayonnaise
1 tbsp heavy cream
2 tsps chopped parsley
2 tsps chopped dill pickles
2 tsps chopped capers
1 tsp chopped onion

Pizza Marinara

PREPARATION TIME:	15 minutes
COOKING TIME:	25-30 minutes
OVEN TEMPERATURE:	425°F (220°C)
SERVES:	4 people

1 cup flour, sifted
1 tsp baking powder
½ tsp salt
⅓ cup milk
2 tbsp salad oil
½ cup canned tomatoes

1 tsp tomato paste
1 clove crushed garlic
½ tsp oregano
½ tsp basil
Fennel seeds
Salt
Pepper
¼ cup shrimp
4 anchovies
¼ cup clams
6-8 mussels
1 tsp capers
2-3 black olives
6 slices mozzarella cheese

Sift flour, baking powder and salt into a bowl and add milk and oil. Stir vigorously until mixture leaves the sides of the bowl. Press it into a ball and knead it in the bowl for about 2 minutes until smooth. Cover, and leave it to sit while preparing sauce. Put tomatoes, tomato paste, herbs, seasoning and garlic together in a small saucepan. Bring to the boil and reduce to thicken. Leave to cool. Roll out the pizza into a 12″ circle. Spread the sauce evenly, leaving a ½″ border around the edge. Scatter over the

This page: Anchovy Pâté with Crudités.
Facing page: Goujons (top) and Pizza Marinara (bottom).

Curry Sauce
2 tbsps mayonnaise
1 tbsp heavy cream
1 tsp curry powder
1½ tsps mango relish

Tomato Herb Sauce
2 tbsps mayonnaise
1 tbsp heavy cream
1 tsp chopped parsley
1 tsp chopped tarragon
1 tsp chopped chives
1 tsp tomato paste
Squeeze of lemon

Fillet the sole and skin the fillets. Rinse fillets in cold water and pat dry. Cut each fillet on the diagonal into pieces about ½″ thick and 2½-3″ long. Coat thoroughly with seasoned flour, shaking off any excess. Beat eggs lightly and mix in the olive oil. Dip fish pieces into the mixture and roll them in the breadcrumbs. Put fish aside in a cool place: do not coat the fish too soon before cooking. Mix ingredients for the various sauces together and set aside. Heat oil in a deep fryer to about 375°F (190°C). Put fish in the frying basket and lower into the hot oil. Fry for 2-3 minutes until crisp and golden brown. Fry in small batches. Drain fish on crumpled paper towels, sprinkle lightly with salt, and then pile the fish into a hot serving dish. Garnish with wedges of lemon and sprigs of parsley, if desired, and serve the sauces separately for dipping the fish.

Shrimp Risotto

PREPARATION TIME: 15 minutes	
COOKING TIME: 25 minutes	
SERVES: 4 people	

1lb unpeeled shrimp
4 tomatoes
3 cloves garlic
1 large onion
3 tbsps olive oil
2 tbsps chopped parsley
1 glass white wine
1½ cups round Italian or risotto rice
1 tsp tomato paste
2 tbsps grated Parmesan cheese
Salt
Freshly ground pepper

Skin, seed and chop tomatoes, and peel and chop garlic and onion. Peel shrimp, leaving 4 unpeeled for garnish. Cook wine and shrimp shells together and leave to cool. Heat olive oil in a fairly wide pan or sauté pan. Soften onion in the oil without browning. Add garlic and parsley. Fry gently for a minute.

Add rice and strain on the wine. Add tomato paste and more water to just barely cover rice. Season with salt and pepper, stirring the rice, adding more water as it becomes absorbed. The rice will take about 20 minutes to cook. When it is cooked, toss in the peeled shrimp and cheese to heat through. Pile risotto into a serving dish and top with unpeeled shrimp. Sprinkle over some chopped parsley.

Sardine Savories

PREPARATION TIME: 10-20 minutes	
COOKING TIME: 20 minutes	
OVEN TEMPERATURE: 375°F (190°C)	
SERVES: 4 people	

8oz pie or puff pastry
¼ cup fresh Parmesan or Cheddar cheese
4oz (approx) canned sardines
Cayenne pepper
Chopped chives or green onion
1 egg, beaten
Salt
Pepper

Prepare the pastry, or use ready-made. Roll it out and cut into 8 pieces large enough to fold up around the sardines. Remove bones from the sardines and put the fillets on top of one half of the pastry rectangles. Sprinkle over the grated cheese, Cayenne pepper, seasoning, and chives or onion, and fold the other half of the pastry over to cover the sardines. Seal the edges well and cut two slits in the top. Brush with the beaten egg and bake until golden brown and risen. Serve hot or cold.

Omelette of Clams and Mussels

PREPARATION TIME: 5 minutes	
COOKING TIME: 7-10 minutes	
SERVES: 4 people	

½ pint shelled clams
½ pint shelled mussels
6-8 eggs
2½ tbsps butter
Drop of anchovy paste
Cayenne pepper
Salt
Pepper
Finely chopped parsley and chives

Poach mussels in boiling salted water for about 2 minutes. Add a bay leaf if desired. Rinse clams under cold water. Separate eggs and beat yolks with anchovy paste, Cayenne pepper and seasoning. Whisk whites until stiff but not dry and fold into yolks. Heat the butter in a large omelette pan and when foaming, pour in the egg mixture. Allow eggs to set on the bottom. Score the omelette down the middle. Add clams and mussels and fold in two. Heat through for 2 minutes to cook the inside of the omelette and to warm the shellfish. Serve immediately, sprinkled with finely chopped parsley and chives. (This dish can be adapted to make individual omelettes).

Kedgeree

PREPARATION TIME: 15 minutes	
COOKING TIME: 20 minutes	
SERVES: 4 people	

¾lb smoked haddock (finnan haddie)
½ cup mushrooms
4oz peeled shrimp
Juice of half a lemon
¾ cup rice
1 small onion
2 cups milk
2 tbsps flour
4 tbsps butter
½ tsp curry powder
4 hard-boiled eggs
Fresh parsley
½ cup cream
Salt
Pepper

Cook rice for about 12 minutes. Drain under hot water to remove starch and leave to dry. Melt butter in a large pan. Slice the onion and fry until golden brown. Add mushrooms and fry for a few seconds before adding the flour. Add curry powder and cook for a minute or two. Gradually work in the cold milk until all is incorporated. Simmer for 5 minutes, stirring constantly, until thick. Skin smoked haddock, cut into small pieces, add to the sauce and continue to cook. Once cooked, add the lemon juice, shrimp and salt and pepper to taste. Stir in the rice. If sauce seems too thick, add cream. Mound kedgeree into a heated serving dish. Sprinkle on chopped parsley and garnish with slices or quarters of egg.

Omelette of Clams and
Mussels (left) and Sardine
Savories (below).

Index